From Experience to Knowledge in ELT

Also published in
Oxford Handbooks for Language Teachers

From Experience to Knowledge in ELT

JULIAN EDGE

SUE GARTON

OXFORD
UNIVERSITY PRESS

OXFORD
UNIVERSITY PRESS

Great Clarendon Street, Oxford ox2 6DP

Oxford University Press is a department of the University of Oxford.
It furthers the University's objective of excellence in research, scholarship,
and education by publishing worldwide in

Oxford New York

Auckland Cape Town Dar es Salaam Hong Kong Karachi
Kuala Lumpur Madrid Melbourne Mexico City Nairobi
New Delhi Shanghai Taipei Toronto

With offices in

Argentina Austria Brazil Chile Czech Republic France Greece
Guatemala Hungary Italy Japan Poland Portugal Singapore
South Korea Switzerland Thailand Turkey Ukraine Vietnam

OXFORD and OXFORD ENGLISH are registered trade marks of
Oxford University Press in the UK and in certain other countries

© Oxford University Press 2009

The moral rights of the authors have been asserted

Database right Oxford University Press (maker)

First published 2009
2012
10 9 8 7 6 5 4

ISBN 978 0 19 442271 0

Typeset by SPI Publisher Services, Pondicherry, India

Printed in China

This book is printed on paper from certified and well-managed sources.

To Karolina, as she makes her own way.
To Enzo, per tutti.

CONTENTS

ACKNOWLEDGEMENTS

Photos reproduced with kind permission from: Agence France Presse 145 (traffic/ Dominic Burke); Alamy 46 (mobile phone/D. Hurst); Corbis 144 (bristlecone pine/D.S. Robins), Cyclepods Ltd 118 (cycle stand); Getty Images 145 (old women/Z. Kulunzny), 151 (man with laptop/Bilderlounge), 58 (man at reception); Getty Images/Foodpix 95 (cooked prawns/Burke/Triolo Productions); Oxford University Press 145 (the OED image is reprinted by permission of the Secretary to the Delegates of Oxford University Press); Powerstock Superstock 144 (disaster); Roberstock.com 145 (plane/L. Smith); Jodi Waxman/OUP 95 (student visitor greeted), 95 (student visitor in bedroom).

Illustrations in extracts by: Stephan Conlin 58 (town plan); Phil Disley 148 (distracted driver), 110 ('Welcome to Folkestone'); Martha Gavin 120 (noisy party neighbours); Harry Venning 94 ('I look just like my father'). All other illustrations by Chris Pavely.

'Popular opinions about language learning and teaching' on page 7 reproduced with kind permission from Patsy M. Lightbown and Nina Spada.

'Weather Report' chant on page 25 reproduced with kind permission from Carolyn Graham.

Before it took its own direction, this book had started life as a revision and updating of *Essentials of English Language Teaching*. It has come a long way since then, but an overall attitude and framework, along with some of the basic content, has survived. Plus ça change…

Our sincere thanks to Nur Kurtoğlu-Hooton for her dedicated collegiality and her comments on an earlier draft of this book.

INTRODUCTION

Who is this book for?

This book is for people who:

- are keen to teach and eager to learn
- realize that their own previous and continuing experience plays an important role in what they learn and how they teach
- recognize that *learning* from experience involves more than just *having* experience
- believe that understanding a situation is more important than abstract theory, but that learning new concepts and terminology can help them to understand a situation better
- want to turn their experience (as language learners and teachers) into knowledge, so as to improve the quality of their future teaching.

If you recognize yourself in any of the above, this book is for you.

About theory and practice

You may often hear a teacher say, *It's all right in theory, but it doesn't work in practice*. However, as authors and teachers, our position is that, if something is not *useful in practice*, then it is *not all right in theory*, either. In fact, this book moves away completely from the view that teaching is about applying theories. The position taken here is that:

- good practice is central
- practice can always be improved
- the most likely way for teachers to improve practice is to understand their experience of it
- to understand this experience, teachers need to be able to talk about it
- to talk about practice, they need to learn relevant concepts and terminology
- as they talk about their practice in new terms, teachers build their practical knowledge out of their experience

- this process of expressing and extending their understanding enables them to develop their theories of what is happening
- on the basis of this expanding knowledge, teachers can improve their practice.

So, this book does *not* ask teachers to *apply theory*. What it does propose is that it can be personally and professionally liberating to *theorize one's practice*, in the sense of understanding and questioning the whys and wherefores of experience. The book aims to involve its readers in that process of developing in tandem what we know and what we do.

Good practice, but no best way

When we say that there is no single 'best way' of teaching English, that does not mean that each teacher has to start from scratch, as though there were no agreement on what counts as good teaching. This book, therefore, gives examples of a variety of reliable teaching methods related to sound principles. It makes suggestions, gives advice, and recommends titles for further reading.

On a daily basis, however, each teacher has to make appropriate decisions for his or her own particular classrooms. Good practice is an interaction among *people* in a *situation*, guided by teachers who use their intelligence, experience, knowledge, skills, sensitivity, creativity, and awareness to help other people learn.

In order to do that, you need to understand why this book makes the suggestions that it does, and on what basis you might want to move away from them. So, having offered reliable methods that you can depend on and alternatives for you to try out, we also introduce ways of thinking about the work that will help you develop your own style. You can make the book even more useful by doing the review activities at the end of each chapter.

About terminology, tests, and materials

The book is not tied down to any specific course or exam, but there is advice on classroom observation and on how to write about teaching, as well as explicit HIGHLIGHTING in the index of key concepts, as tested by the Cambridge ESOL Teacher Knowledge Test.

The expression, English Language Teaching, and its abbreviation, ELT, is used throughout the book to cover what is also referred to as Teaching English as a Foreign Language (TEFL), Teaching English as a Second Language (TESL), and Teaching English to Speakers of Other Languages (TESOL).

The examples used have been taken from genuine classroom interaction and actual published materials wherever possible, but some examples have been

made up where either brevity or clarity seemed the more important considerations. The convention of using * to indicate non-standard English usage
has been used throughout. Words in small capitals in the text are listed in the
Glossary at the end of the book.

An open invitation

Teaching English to speakers of other languages in the twenty-first century
is a global activity that requires local sensitivity in order to be at its best. In a
similar spirit, this book is offered as a common basis for particular individual
and collegial growth. The authors hope that it will help you establish the
teaching identity you wish for, both in your own professional context and as
a member of the international ELT community.

PART ONE

Familiarization

The first part of this book explores the English Language Teaching (ELT) classroom in order to examine what is to be found there. The main elements of ELT in any situation are:

- the people
- the processes of language learning and teaching
- aspects of the language itself
- the language learning materials usually available
- the classroom environment and kinds of equipment you might use.

At the same time, the way in which these elements are involved in practical teaching techniques will also be considered.

In one sense, you know all this already from your experience of such classrooms, either as a language learner, or as a language teacher, or both. But if you investigate that experience more carefully, what more might you learn?

While you work on the ideas in this book, think about the actual details of your own situation, or of situations you have known. Do the ideas in the book match up with your experience? Can you be specific?

The activities at the end of each chapter also summarize the chapter. They are meant to help you enrich your reading with your experience and enrich your experience with your reading. They will be of most use if you have a friend or colleague to discuss them with. In that way, you can develop your ideas as you talk and listen.

1 PEOPLE

This chapter looks at the people most obviously involved in ELT: learners and teachers. We start by looking at similarities and differences among learners wherever they are in the world and what this means for teachers. We then go on to look at teachers and the roles they take on in the ELT classroom.

Learners

All learners are the same: outside the classroom, they have a family, friends, work, study or play, responsibilities, a place to live, and all the joys and sorrows that come with those things. They bring into the classroom their names, their knowledge, experience, intelligence, skills, emotions, imagination, awareness, creativity, sense of humour, problems, purposes, dreams, hopes, aspirations, fears, memories, interests, blind spots, prejudices, habits, expectations, likes, dislikes, preferences, and everything else that goes with being a human being, including the ability to speak at least one language.

In all these ways, however, each learner is also individual and different. No two learners have the same knowledge, skills, or expectations, or any of the other things listed in the last paragraph. Learners are also influenced by their age, by their educational, social, and cultural backgrounds, and by their preferred LEARNING STYLES, which they may or may not share with their fellow students and teacher.

Age

It is often thought that children are more successful at learning languages than adults. According to the critical age hypothesis, for example, there is a period up to around 12–13 years of age when children learn a language most easily. After that period, it is said, success in language learning will be limited. However, that is not necessarily true if we are talking about learning a language formally, in a classroom. It also depends on what is meant by 'successful'. While children may ACQUIRE a 'native-like' accent whereas older learners usually do not, that is obviously not the only measure of success. Success can also be measured in terms of how well a learner can communicate or make him or herself understood. If learners have very specific activities they need to carry out in English, such as giving a business presentation, success can also be measured in terms of how well they can do those specific things. (See Brown 2007 for a detailed discussion of these issues.)

Of course teachers have to take the age of their learners into account. Younger learners have shorter attention spans and need to be given more and shorter activities to hold their interest. Teenagers, on the other hand, may be more likely to feel embarrassed if they think they are not very proficient in the language. They may feel inadequate and frustrated when they cannot say what they want to. So they may need activities which have a clear outcome and which give them a sense of achievement.

Younger learners are unlikely to learn through explanations of grammar rules and doing grammar exercises, but they will learn through stories and play. Older learners and adults especially may prefer the systematic structure that rules of grammar give.

Education

The educational background of the learners may also influence how they learn. Some education systems place emphasis on rote learning (memorizing) and input from the teacher. Learners who come from such a background are unlikely to find the sort of LEARNER INDEPENDENCE and AUTONOMY often encouraged in ELT helpful to their language learning, at least not without the time and support (or LEARNER TRAINING) necessary for them to see how such an approach might work for them.

Culture

Learners come from cultural backgrounds where the role of English is different, and bring with them differing attitudes to learning English. Some learners may be highly motivated and very happy to learn English. Others may feel that they have no alternative, because without English, they may be marginalized in today's global world. They may feel forced to learn English and feel resentful as a result; this will negatively affect their motivation. (See Chapter 2 for a more detailed discussion of motivation.)

Learning styles

Individual learners prefer to learn things in different ways. In other words, they have different learning styles. For example, some people are essentially auditory learners, so they learn better when they hear things spoken aloud. They may prefer to learn through listening to dialogues or hearing the teacher

MODEL new language. Others are basically visual learners, who learn better when they see things written down, or as pictures. They prefer to learn through reading or watching the teacher write on the board. Finally, some people are essentially kinaesthetic learners – they prefer to learn by doing things. They like to move around, carry out projects, or have the teacher demonstrate language through objects or physical movement. Individual learners have differing mixes of these three tendencies, so teachers need to try and cater for these different learning styles in their classrooms.

Whatever the variables, some learners are more successful than others. Good language learners often have the following learner characteristics in common, although no individual learner would have them all. Typically such learners:

- have a positive attitude to the language they want to learn and to speakers of that language
- have a strong personal motivation to learn the language
- are confident that they will be successful learners
- are prepared to risk making mistakes and learn from them
- like learning about the language
- organize their own practice of the language
- find ways to say things when they do not know how to express them correctly
- willingly get into situations where the language is being used, and use it as often as they can
- work directly in the language rather than translate from their first language (L1)
- think about their strategies for learning and remembering, and consciously try out new strategies.

As teachers, we try to teach all our students, but the successful learners are usually those who take on some responsibility for their own learning.

Teachers

What can teachers learn from what we have said so far about learners?

First, a sensitive teacher who takes into account the characteristics of different learners can create the conditions in the classroom where the greatest number of learners can be successful.

Second, therefore, learners should not be seen as language-learning machines, nor should language learning be seen only as an intellectual process. Learners, as whole human beings, may have many other things on their minds; all the similarities and differences between them listed above are frequently expressed through language and can all be used to enrich language learning. To learn a language is to learn to express oneself.

Third, teachers have to make an effort to inform themselves about their learners. If teachers share a cultural and linguistic background with their learners, this can be an advantage. If not, the teacher needs to show an explicit interest in gaining such knowledge. Teachers have to be sensitive to social and cultural distinctions among their learners and try to be open to the personal needs, learning styles, and reasons for learning of their individual students.

Fourth, classrooms should be places where the characteristics of good learners are discussed and encouraged. Individuals can then be helped to discover positive characteristics which suit their own personality, society and culture. Some learners, for instance, will learn better through EXPOSURE to natural language, while others will learn better through self-study and practice. You will need to work closely with your students to help them find the balance that suits them as individuals.

Teacher success can be measured most obviously by how much their students learn. Like learners, however, all teachers are different, and for just the same reason: they are whole human beings with an individual mixture of all the elements listed above in relation to learners. Two important insights arise from this:

1 The best teacher that any one individual can be will in some ways be different from the best teacher that anyone else can be, as each teacher invests his or her strengths and develops his or her potential.
2 It is important to recognize from the start that no teacher is likely simply to be a 'good teacher' in a general sense. You may be a great teacher for some students, an average teacher for others, and nevertheless, despite all your skills and flexibility, be seen as a poor teacher by yet others. The challenge is to go on developing into the teacher you most want to be.

Teacher characteristics

The way teachers teach is profoundly influenced by what they believe about how languages are learnt and how they should be taught. For example, teachers who believe that learners learn best when they are engaged and interested in what they are doing may make more use of games and extended speaking activities, such as debates and role plays in the classroom. Teachers who believe that learners learn best when they are given clear explanations of rules may make more use of FOCUS ON FORM activities.

Beliefs about learning and teaching can be the result of past experiences:

● as a language learner
● of being taught by others
● of teacher education courses
● as a teacher in a particular educational context.

Whatever the reasons for your beliefs, it is always a good idea to reflect on what you believe about language teaching and learning, and how this affects the way you teach. Here is an example of a questionnaire that helps you to think about your beliefs:

Popular opinions about language learning and teaching

Indicate the extent to which you agree with each statement by marking an X at the appropriate point on the line between 'strongly agree' and 'strongly disagree'.

1   Languages are learned mainly through imitation.
    strongly agree ___|___|___X___|___|___ strongly disagree

2   Parents usually correct young children when they make grammatical errors.
    strongly agree ___|___|___|X|___|___ strongly disagree

3   Highly intelligent people are good language learners.
    strongly agree ___|___|___|___|X|___ strongly disagree

4   The most important predictor of success in second language acquisition is motivation.
    strongly agree X|___|___|___|___|___ strongly disagree

5   The earlier a second language is introduced in school programmes, the greater the likelihood of success in learning.
    strongly agree ___|X|___|___|___|___ strongly disagree

6   Most of the mistakes that second language learners make are due to interference from their first language.
    strongly agree ___|X|___|___|___|___ strongly disagree

7   The best way to learn new vocabulary is through reading.
    strongly agree X|___|___|___|___|___ strongly disagree

8   It is essential for learners to be able to pronounce all the individual sounds in the second language.
    strongly agree X|___|___|___|___|___ strongly disagree

9   Once learners know roughly 1000 words and the basic structure of a language, they can easily participate in conversations with native speakers.
    strongly agree ___|___|___X|___|___ strongly disagree

10 Teachers should present grammatical rules one at a time, and learners should practise examples of each one before going on to another.
    strongly agree X|___|___|___|___|___ strongly disagree

11 Teachers should teach simple language structures before complex ones.
    strongly agree X|___|___|___|___|___ strongly disagree

12 Learners' errors should be corrected as soon as they are made in order to prevent the formation of bad habits.
    strongly agree X|___|___|___|___|___ strongly disagree

13 Teachers should use materials that expose students to only those language structures they have already been taught.
    strongly agree ___|___|___|___|X___ strongly disagree

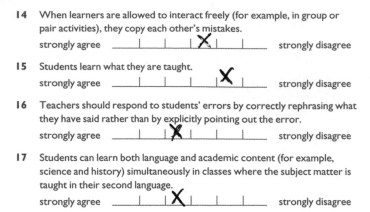

14   When learners are allowed to interact freely (for example, in group or pair activities), they copy each other's mistakes.

strongly agree ____|____|____|X__|____|____ strongly disagree

15   Students learn what they are taught.

strongly agree ____|____|____|X__|____ strongly disagree

16   Teachers should respond to students' errors by correctly rephrasing what they have said rather than by explicitly pointing out the error.

strongly agree ____|____|X__|____|____|____ strongly disagree

17   Students can learn both language and academic content (for example, science and history) simultaneously in classes where the subject matter is taught in their second language.

strongly agree ____|____|X__|____|____|____ strongly disagree

Figure 1.1 Popular opinions about language learning and teaching (Lightbown and Spada, 2006, page xvii-xviii)

One important thing for all teachers to remember is that the differences present an opportunity to learn from each other. If you find that you yourself sometimes reject people's ideas as boring or uninspiring, take time to consider that some people might have a much better sense than you do of organization and progression through a series of lessons (see Chapter 6.) If you sometimes reject other teachers' ideas as too fanciful or unrealistic, consider that they may have a greater talent than you do for imagining what might be possible. You may still want to disagree, but bear in mind that:

- A useful technique for you might not be so useful for someone else, and vice versa.
- The difference between 'a practical suggestion' and 'just a theoretical idea' might lie in you.

Teacher roles

Whatever you believe about teaching and learning, one inescapable fact about the language classroom remains – the teacher is the most powerful person there, and one with many different roles to play.

Of the many things any teacher has to do, these are the most important:

Organizing

One of the most important roles of the teacher is that of organizer of what goes on in the classroom, so that the learners feel their activity is purposeful, and that they are putting their efforts into a framework they can trust. Learners need just enough structure to feel supported, and just enough freedom to feel they have room to grow (Stevick 1980).

Consequently the teacher needs to make sure that the lesson is planned sufficiently carefully to move forward in a relatively ordered way, and that the transition from one activity to the next is clear. One way the teacher organizes what happens is by giving instructions so that the learners know what activity they are supposed to be doing and how they are supposed to be doing it. Language such as the following (where the teacher tells the whole class what to do and organizes an example for them to follow), is commonly heard in the ELT classroom:

TEACHER   Last Tuesday we did a lesson on work and do you remember the name of that company in Brazil?
STUDENT   Semco
TEACHER   Semco that's right, and we had quite a good exercise on work expressions, words, or phrases and expressions to do with work, OK? So what I'm going to do is quite simple. I'm going to read to you definitions of some of these words and I want you to see if you can just write down what you think the word or phrase is, OK? We'll do one as an example, so you know what I'm talking about.

The teacher in this example not only gives the instructions for the activity, but also uses the opportunity to remind her learners of what they did in their previous lesson, and then involves them directly in this by eliciting the name of the company they had studied.

Providing security

If learners feel safe, they are better able to take part in the lesson. If they feel that everyone in the class, including the teacher, is on the same side, they may be prepared to risk making mistakes they can learn from.

The learners in the example below had been asked to make up the title for a reading passage. We can see how the teacher encourages one group by asking them to give their title because it was 'good', even if the language is not entirely correct. The humour and laughter show that the atmosphere is very relaxed and the learners seem to be enjoying the lesson:

TEACHER   Oh, and yours was good as well.
MARIO   The Greek diet allows villagers to survive to a good age for smokers too. *(Learners and teacher all laugh.)*
TEACHER   *(laughing)* Important element.
PATRIZIA Do you smoke?
MARIO   Yes.
PATRIZIA Yeah. *(Learners and teacher all laugh.)*

Motivating

Some learners will be motivated to learn for external reasons, which helps greatly, but all learners also need to feel involved in class work. This happens best when they are motivated by interesting tasks, when they experience success, and when they see the relevance of class work to their outside lives.

Informing

Learners need to be *told* things, and *told how to do* them. Here a learner has used the phrase 'such loud party' and the teacher is explaining why this is incorrect:

> TEACHER   Here we say *it's such a loud party* because 'party' is a singular noun and it's a countable noun. You can't just say 'party', you have to add an article or something. The same thing if you say 'it was such a beautiful day', for example.

Modelling

Learners need to be *shown* things, and *shown how to do* them. In the following example, we see the teacher modelling the target form of the language. At the same time, she is also giving information about the language by explaining the rules. In this respect, teachers often play more than one role at the same time:

> TEACHER   So, what *were* the people like? We use the verb *to be*, OK? Here people are plural, so the verb is the plural form. The question word *what*: *What were the people like?* The *like* comes always at the end of the sentence – of the question, and you can use this form to ask about all things. *What were the people like?*

Giving feedback

Learners need to know how close they are getting to their targets. Was that meaning clear? Was the verb correct? The next example follows on from the previous one and shows how the teacher gives learners FEEDBACK on their attempts to use the new target form:

> MARIA   What were the food like?
> TEACHER   Food is singular.
> PAOLA   Was
> TEACHER   That's right. Good.
> MARIA   What was the weather like?
> TEACHER   That's right. *What was the food like? What was the weather like?*

Guiding

Learners need a helping hand to discover new things and to practise new skills. As we saw in the previous example, giving feedback can be one form of guidance.

Monitoring

When learners are working on their own, or in pairs and groups, they need to know that they are doing what they are supposed to be doing. They may also need help to complete the task. In the example below, the learners are working in pairs, with one learner trying to work out grammar rules from example sentences and the other from explanations of the rules. They then have to compare what they have found. The teacher is MONITORING to make sure the pairs know what they are supposed to be doing, but she is also guiding them towards the answers:

TEACHER   Right, who's going to look at the examples and who's going to read the rule? Then is it you? OK, you read the rule and you look at the examples.
(Teacher moves to another pair.)
TEACHER   Right, who's looking at the rule? You, Filippo? Then you don't look at the rule, Paolo, you just look at that part.
(Teacher moves to another pair.)
TEACHER   Ah, are you both looking at the explanation?
(Teacher moves to another pair.)
TEACHER   Are you OK?
MARIO   I have written 'to use *so* when you have a noun and *such* when you have a pronoun' but it's wrong.
TEACHER   Well, you're on the right track. It's a good idea.

Encouraging

Learners need to feel that the language is developing inside them, even if what they are producing at the moment seems unlike standard English. In addition to explicit encouraging, as in the previous example, this also means not correcting learners all the time, but encouraging them to communicate with whatever language resources they have, when it is appropriate to do so, as in the following:

MIRCO   Coffee is good.
TEACHER   Not too much.
MIRCO   Three, four …
TEACHER   Only one or two.
MIRCO   No. Three, four, five …
TEACHER   Yeah.
NICO   Coffee Italian is good.
(Teacher and learners laugh.)
NICO   English coffee, ugh.
TEACHER   But Italian coffee's very strong.
NICO   Strong.

Evaluating

Some learners have external standards that must be reached, important examinations to pass. Teachers need to evaluate learners in order to let them know where they stand, what they have achieved, and what they still need to do.

So, are the roles of the teacher to organize, provide security, motivate, instruct, model, guide, monitor, inform, explain, give feedback, encourage, and evaluate?

Yes, indeed. But the best teachers do something else as well. In a way that suits the individuals, society, and culture concerned, they encourage learners to take on some responsibility themselves in these areas. The aim is to help learners become independent of teachers, so that learners can use what they learn and continue to learn on their own.

Finally, there is one important feature of teaching we need to mention: teachers almost always work alone. This is unfortunate, because inviting a colleague to watch you teach, or watching a colleague yourself, can be a very worthwhile learning experience. A difficulty arises as soon as the word 'observation' is mentioned because observation is usually associated with being assessed and tends to carry with it the fear of criticism or failure. But this does not have to be. The single most important change we can hope for in teaching is for teachers who trust each other to visit each other's classrooms and be present, not to evaluate, but to share. The sooner you start, the easier it is, and the more you will learn. We return to this topic in Chapter 11, but one such sharing activity is suggested in the questions and activities below. We hope you find it intriguing enough to try out.

Summary

In this chapter, we have emphasized the importance of thinking about learners and teachers as whole people whose individuality can be a source of learning. We have looked at the similarities and differences between learners and at what makes a good language learner. We have also examined the similarities and differences between language teachers and the various roles they have to take on in the classroom. The questions and activities which follow are designed to help you review and reflect on the chapter in personal terms.

Questions and activities

Think about your responses and then discuss them with a colleague if possible.

1 What do you think about the idea of bringing the learners' outside life into the classroom? Have you any ideas or experience of how this can be done?

2 Look at the characteristics of good language learners on page 5. Do you recognize them? Are they true of you? Are they true of good language learners you have known? Can you think of any other characteristics of good language learners?

3   Answer the questions in the Lightbown and Spada questionnaire on pages 7–8. What do you learn from it in terms of your beliefs about learning and teaching?

4   Who were the best teachers you have had? What was so good about them? Did it have anything to do with their way of treating you as a person? Can you relate their teaching to the list of things on page 12 that need to be taken care of in class?

5   Look at that list again. One way to help learners move towards independence is for the teacher to share the responsibility for these areas with them. Would that be possible in your situation? If so, how?

6   Find someone you can trust and ask him or her to watch you teach. Afterwards, tell your observer two things that you feel went well. Your observer does not need to tell you anything. (See Chapter 11 page 174 if you would like to know the rationale for this.) You will be surprised how much you can learn!

(For answers, thoughts, and comments on these questions, see page 183.)

2 LEARNING AND TEACHING PROCESSES

The people we see in the ELT classroom are involved in processes that teachers need to understand. In this chapter, we start by establishing the learner's task in terms of communicative behaviour. We then look at the three levels of mental processing involved in foreign language learning, and the two basic approaches to language teaching available. Finally, cutting across these two basic approaches we examine five elements of response that ELT has developed to support language learning. These ideas underlie the methodological suggestions that follow throughout the book.

Language learning

The learners' task

Language learners find themselves with multiple demands on their attention. The learners' task might be described as learning to juggle these different demands, as they learn to communicate and meet the need for:

- *Accuracy*: conforming to the language system itself
- *Fluency*: operating the system quickly
- *Appropriacy*: using the language successfully in different situations and with different people
- *Flexibility*: not being put off by difficulties in any of the above, whether their own or other people's.

The teacher's task is, of course, to facilitate this learning. The connection between learning and teaching is not a simple one, but a good place to start is to examine what we know about language learning itself. Lightbown and Spada (2006) provide an excellent overview of this area. What follows here are the basic points from a teaching perspective.

Our brain works for us at three different levels, the subconscious, the conscious, and the metaconscious. In the context of language learning, we can identify three relevant outcomes:

First, people sometimes learn language subconsciously, by 'picking it up'. This is typically the case when learners are in a situation where they are exposed to natural language use in meaningful social interaction. This kind of informal language ACQUISITION tends to encourage oral FLUENCY in the language, as well as a natural feel for what is socially APPROPRIATE and INAPPROPRIATE.

There is some evidence that learners seem to acquire the grammar of any language in more or less the same sequence: there is a natural order in which language develops along its own path. The level of formal ACCURACY achieved depends on the demands made on the learner to become more accurate, according to what he or she wants to achieve.

Second, people also learn language consciously, through formal study, as is frequently the case in most classrooms. In this situation, learners study the language in the sequence in which it is presented to them, usually following an organized SYLLABUS. This kind of learning tends to encourage accuracy in the language, as well as knowledge of what is correct. Learners develop their fluency and feeling for what is socially appropriate in the language in other contexts, according to the actual demands made on them to communicate in meaningful situations.

Third, in addition to the two cognitive processes described above, human beings work metacognitively. In other words, adult learners in particular have analytical skills that enable them to think about their learning, monitor their progress, and guide their actions. As we said in Chapter 1, good language learners think about their learning strategies (see below) and consciously try out different strategies. This kind of learning allows learners to become more independent as they gain insight into how they learn and what does and does not work well for them.

These two types of cognitive process, together with metacognitive thinking, can also support each other. For example, when you acquire naturally a new way of saying something in a foreign language, you might later analyse the language and think about how that segment of language works grammatically. On the other hand, when you are studying one area of a language, you may pick up some other element of the language without being aware of it at the time. Some have argued (for example, Krashen 1982) that what is learnt consciously and what is learnt subconsciously play completely different and separate roles in the learner's ability to communicate, but there is no convincing evidence for this. The important thing is that teachers try to stimulate subconscious, conscious, and metaconscious mental activity in their learners.

As we said in Chapter 1, it would be a mistake to think of language learning as just an intellectual process. However learners learn and whatever mental level they are working at, they are more likely to be successful if they are motivated to engage with the language and with people who speak the language.

Motivation

Learners learn a language for different reasons. On the one hand, some have an external reason for learning. They may have chosen to learn English because they need it for further study, or for their jobs (either for their day-to-day work or to achieve promotion); these learners are said to be extrinsically motivated. On the other hand, there are learners who choose to learn a language simply because they want to, without any particular need; these learners are intrinsically motivated. Another common way of talking about motivation is to distinguish between instrumental motivation (for example, when people want to use the language as a tool to achieve a specific purpose), and integrative motivation when people want to integrate into a society (as is often the immigrant experience). Globalization has also meant that many learners may be motivated by the idea of integration into the international body of English users.

But what about those learners who have no choice in the matter, such as the millions of schoolchildren all over the world? It is the teacher's job to help them either to identify some extrinsic motivation (whether instrumental or integrative), or to awaken some intrinsic motivation, or both. It is thus the teacher's responsibility to try to ensure that lessons are interesting and stimulating enough to encourage these learners to want to learn.

It is precisely because motivation is so central to language learning that this difficult aspect of the teacher's work is so important. Teachers need to try to find out why their learners are learning the language, what they need to learn, how they prefer to learn, what they are interested in, and what they might become interested in.

If you are able to make these GOALS, NEEDS, preferences, and possibilities work together, you are more likely to have motivated learners to work with, and they are more likely to learn.

Language teaching

Two broad approaches

In terms of broad approach, there are two ways to teach people to use a language:

1 Move from communication to language. That is, you:

- create a situation in which the students want to communicate something
- encourage them to communicate as best they can
- focus their attention on the language forms used to achieve communication (if this seems necessary).

This approach, which moves from meaning to form, starts with subconscious learning and shifts to conscious learning. The clearest form of this approach is what is called task-based learning (TBL). In a TBL approach, the students are given a task to complete, possibly preceded by a pre-task to prepare them for it. Students carry out the task with whatever language resources they have; the aim is simply to complete the task. In the final stage, students focus on some aspects of the language used, usually in the form of activities which draw their attention to features of the language, how it is formed, and how it is used, thereby increasing their language awareness. TBL is just one example of a general meaning-to-form approach. These approaches will be discussed in detail in Chapter 7.

2 Move from language to communication by combining the different elements of the language that have been isolated for learning. Item by item, you:

- provide a model of the item(s) of language to be learnt (the TARGET LANGUAGE of the lesson)
- get the students to copy and practise the model
- encourage the students to PERSONALIZE the model by using it to communicate something they want to say.

This approach, which moves from form to meaning, starts with conscious learning and shifts to subconscious learning. The clearest form of this is an approach often referred to as Presentation, Practice, and Production (PPP). In this approach, the teacher models and explains the language point to be taught, usually through a short reading or listening text. The learners then practise the language point through exercises which carefully control the language they use. Finally, the learners are given more open activities where they can use the language point more freely and internalize it for future use.

Again, PPP is just one way of implementing a form-to-meaning approach. We discuss it and other approaches in Chapter 8.

As a person, you might develop a preference for one approach over the other. As a teacher however, you need to make sure that you combine both approaches in order to be fair to the preferences of different students. Some students will dislike copying models, some will dislike being called on to communicate before they have been taught the necessary forms, and some will be confused by any focus on forms without meaningful use.

It is important to remember too that students do not necessarily learn what teachers think they have taught them. They might learn less than the teacher intended in one area, but they might be acquiring something else in another.

By focusing sometimes on language and sometimes on communication, students can take advantage of subconscious and conscious learning. In addition, metacognitive strategies are encouraged by giving them opportunities to reflect on what they are doing and become better learners. Students who are aware of their own preferences and the preferences of others can better appreciate what is happening in class and better support their own learning outside the classroom.

Five basic elements

So far in this chapter we have introduced three levels of mental activity and two general approaches to language teaching. We are now going to examine five basic elements of ELT which have a role to play in both general approaches and which need to be integrated. They arise from different views of language learning, which is why it is easy to discuss them separately. But our interest is not to follow these ideas back to their origins; it is to see how they all support current ELT thinking and how they contribute to fulfilling teaching goals by engaging learning processes. They are: *communication, feelings, rules, practice,* and *strategies*. We find it useful to picture them woven together like strands in a rope, where the combination makes the whole stronger than the sum of its separate parts.

At the end of this chapter, there are some ELT materials which exemplify these different elements.

Communication

Communication is at the centre of ELT, and this section of the chapter relates to all the others which follow. There are two key reasons why communication is so important:

Communication is the goal of language teaching. People usually learn English because for some reason, in some way, they need or want to be able to communicate in English. Even when this is not the case, as with schoolchildren or students following compulsory courses, there can still be some kind of communicative goal to motivate them. This usually involves establishing a connection between the students' everyday lives and the use of English. Examples of such a connection would be:

- being able to sing the words of their favourite pop songs
- reading what an English-language newspaper wrote about their national soccer team, or their government
- listening to a foreigner talk about life in their city
- investigating a problem from their academic discipline.

Communication is part of the learning process. That is to say, communication is not only the *goal*, it is also an important part of the *way*. This is the most important idea at the centre of what is meant by communicative language teaching, and it applies to both broad approaches that we described above:

- Using formally learnt language to communicate helps make it more automatically available for spontaneous use. If, for example, the students have just learnt how to ask questions with the verb *to have,* they can ask their classmates if they have any brothers or sisters. Thus 'Do you have…' might become an automatic set phrase for them.
- During meaningful communication, further segments of language may be acquired subconsciously. To continue with the same example, while students are practising *Do you have*…in 'Do you have any brothers and sisters?' they may acquire this particular and correct use of *any* and develop a feel for its use without explicit teaching.

Communication clearly involves more than language; but here we are going to concentrate on linguistic communication. It is worth pausing to ask what communication is for:

Communication is used in order to get, give, or exchange information, for example:

TEACHER   Nico, how many hours do you work?
NICO   Is depend. I study nine or ten hour a day.

Communication is used in order to do things and get things done. Here, for example, Vittoria makes a request:

TEACHER   Now today I want to look at the conditionals, so if you turn in your textbook to page 74…Yes, sorry?
VITTORIA   May I have the handout from last time, please?
TEACHER   From last time? Of course.

In real communication, one can never be sure what someone is going to say. (See Vittoria's request in the previous example.)

Communication expresses and develops relationships between people. Compare:

I want this ready by 5.30.

with

Do you think you might be able to have this ready by 5.30?

People from different societies and cultures signal different things by what they say and the way they say them. They have different ideas, for example, about politeness. The German who says, *Give me six bread rolls,* in a baker's shop is being perfectly polite in her own terms, but an English shop assistant might not think so, because this sounds to him more like an order than a request.

So, language learners need to know how to:

- exchange information
- get things done

- deal with the unexpected
- establish the kind of relationship they want
- avoid judging other people according to their own values.

The classroom can offer ample opportunities for students to learn and practise all of these life skills.

We must not think that these issues can be seen as separate from the grammar, pronunciation, and other aspects of the language system itself. In the example *Do you think you might be able to have this ready by 5.30?* the relationship indicated is directly connected to the use of the modal verb *might*, the inquiry about possibility, and the choice of a question form rather than a statement. And if students are learning English in order to pass exams or write reports, for instance, they will eventually need to achieve greater formal accuracy if they are going to succeed. Simply 'exchanging information', as Nico does in the first example above, will probably not satisfy their examiners or their bosses.

English language teachers need to be able to relate teaching the English language system to teaching the ability to communicate in English in a way that is appropriate to particular groups of learners. Ideas about communication are at the centre of ELT, as we shall emphasize throughout the rest of this book.

The *communicative* element of ELT relates to conscious and subconscious learning, as well as to accuracy, fluency, appropriacy, and flexibility.

Feelings

We have already mentioned the importance of learner motivation, attitude, confidence, security, and willingness to take risks. There is another reason for our emphasis on the importance of a positive emotional environment in the language class: secure, motivated learners will be prepared to make a personal investment in learning. That is, learners will talk about themselves and about things that matter to them. In this environment, they will also listen with respect to what others have to say. The foreign language then starts to perform the normal FUNCTIONS of language – expressing what people care about and helping them to establish relationships with other people. When language use is as meaningful as this, it is also memorable, so language learning takes place. Positive emotional involvement leads to effective learning.

There are some dangers here, however. Obviously it is not acceptable to pry into people's lives, or in any way oblige people to talk about topics that might be painful for them. The power of 'reality' must be recognized when it can help evoke positive emotion, but it is also necessary to recognize that reality can be hurtful. Two points to remember are:

1 Activities which deal specifically with positive emotions are to be preferred and encouraged.
2 Students must always have some way out of activities they consider too personal. Even talking about a common topic such as the learner's family may be problematic if that family is going through a difficult period, is broken, or is in any way unconventional. It is probably always a good idea at least to give learners the option of using their imagination to invent answers if they prefer.

As long as care is taken, ELT can provide many useful activities (often called humanistic) which call on learners to share personal information through the medium of English. (For examples, see Davis et al. 1999.) Such activities can be effective when used by a sensitive teacher, but they are not magic formulas for making teachers sensitive. When used insensitively, they are powerfully demotivating.

The *feelings* element of ELT relates to subconscious learning, as well as to fluency, appropriacy, and flexibility. It is also connected with the idea that learners must be involved as whole human beings in their language learning.

Rules

The rules we are talking about here are rules which attempt to describe the way English actually *is*, not rules which tell people what they *ought* to say. So we are talking about *descriptive* rules such as:

- The third person singular of the present simple ends with the sound /s/, /z/, or /ɪz/:

  This puppet walks, sings, and dances.

We do not mean *prescriptive* rules of the kind:

- You should not end a sentence with a preposition.

Rules of language are important for one very good reason: a rule is a small thing to learn, but it can have big results. For example, once students have learnt that English makes a past tense by adding –*ed* to a verb, they can make a past tense of any verb they need to use and they will almost certainly be understood, even if the form is not absolutely correct. As they continue to learn, they develop better rules, especially if they pay attention to how the language works, and learn from their mistakes.

It is not enough simply to *tell* students what the rules are. To encourage more active learning and participation, students can be given a rule and asked to use it in producing language. This is known as deductive learning. The activity in Materials extract 2.1 requires students to use deductive learning:

6A	*there is / there are*		
		Singular	Plural
	⊞	**There's** a piano.	**There are** some glasses in the cupboard.
	⊟	**There isn't** a fridge.	**There aren't** any pictures.
	⍰	**Is there** a TV?	**Are there** any glasses?
	✔✘	Yes, **there is**. No, **there isn't**.	Yes, **there are**. No, **there aren't**.

- We often use *there is / are* with *a / an*, *some*, and *any*.
- Use *some* and *any* with plural nouns. *Some* = not an exact number.
- Use *some* in ⊞ sentences and *any* in ⊟ and ⍰.

⚠ Be careful. *There is* and *It is* are different.
There's a key on the table. It's the key to the kitchen.

6A

a Complete the sentences with *There's* or *There are*.

There's _____ a sofa in the living room.
1 _____ four cups in the cupboard.
2 _____ a clock in the kitchen.
3 _____ lots of chairs.
4 _____ a garage.
5 _____ some pictures on the wall.
6 _____ a desk in the study.

b Write ⊞, ⊟, or ⍰ sentences with *there is / are*.

⊞ chairs / the garden *There are some chairs in the garden.*
1 ⊞ table / the kitchen
2 ⍰ fireplace / the living room
3 ⊟ plants / the living room
4 ⍰ cupboards / the kitchen
5 ⊟ shower / bathroom
6 ⊞ shelves / study

Materials extract 2.1 Oxenden, Latham-Koenig, and Seligson: New English File Elementary, pages 132–3

Alternatively, students can be given examples of new language and then *shown* what the rule is. Or they can be given examples and asked to *work out* what the rule is. This is referred to as inductive learning. The activity in Materials extract 2.2 requires students to use inductive learning:

Discussing grammar

3 Work with a partner. What is the difference in meaning in the pairs of sentences below? When does *'d = had*? When does *'d = would*?

1 He asked them how they'd travelled to the wedding.
He asked them how they'd travel to the wedding.

2 She told her mother that she loved John.
She told her mother that she'd love John.

3 She said they lived in Dublin.
She said they'd lived in Dublin.

What did the people actually say in direct speech?

4 Report these sentences.

1 'I'm tired!' he said.
2 'Are you leaving on Friday?' she asked me.
3 'We haven't seen Jack for a long time,' they said.
4 'We flew to Tokyo,' they said.
5 'Which airport did you fly from?' I asked them.
6 'The flight has been cancelled,' the announcement said.
7 'I'll call you later,' he said.
8 'We can't do the exercise,' they told the teacher.

Materials extract 2.2 Soars and Soars: New Headway Plus Intermediate, page 95

Rules need not always be spelled out explicitly; they can often be implicit in other activities. The *rules* element of ELT is related to conscious and metaconscious learning and to accuracy. It is also connected with the idea of involving students in their learning, using their intelligence and creativity.

Practice

The first time anyone tries to do something new, he or she is unlikely to be completely successful. And if they are, it might just be luck! The same goes for language learning. Students need an opportunity to practise new language in an organized way until they are familiar with it and understand how what they have just learnt relates to what they knew before. Practice can take different forms, but broadly speaking it can be seen as ranging from controlled or restricted practice, to less controlled or freer practice.

Controlled practice

In controlled practice of the target language of the lesson, the focus is on accuracy and students have little or no choice in the language that they use.

There are many different types of exercise that can be used to practise language in a controlled way. One type asks students to complete sentences or gaps in sentences with the language they are practising. For example, students might be asked to complete sentences. (See Materials extract 2.1.) Another type of exercise asks students to choose between two alternatives.

Other examples of controlled practice are the various drill techniques. Drills are highly controlled exercises where the teacher provides a PROMPT and the students respond, collectively or individually.

There are a number of different types of drill. In choral drills all the students repeat something together. This type of drill is useful for beginners because it enables them to try out something new without being heard speaking alone. Individual drills are similar to choral drills, but each student responds singly to the teacher's prompt.

Rather than just repeat what the teacher says, students can also be asked to change something in the teacher's prompt. This is the case, for example, with substitution drills. For example:

TEACHER: I went to a party last night: a restaurant. Lee?
LEE: I went to a restaurant last night.

Finally, there are transformation drills, where the teacher provides a prompt and the students have to repeat by changing the prompt in some way, for example, changing the verb form:

TEACHER: They're waiting for the bus: She.... Carla, you, please.
CARLA: She's waiting for the bus.
TEACHER: Good: I.... Now you, Max.
MAX: I'm waiting for the bus.

Some types of drill can be made more fun by turning them into chants. Chants are phrases or sentences that are repeated, using a regular rhythm and are very useful for practising stress and intonation. Here is an example from Graham (2000), which provides practice of the various forms of *will*:

Weather Report
Will it rain today,
or will it snow?
Don't listen to the forecasters,
They don't know,

When the weatherman says,
"We won't have rain,"
we'll probably get a hurricane.

He promised us sunshine,
And what did we get?
We got very, very, wet.

A certain amount of repetition of new language/form helps it to become available at the automatic level. However, while repetition may include some relatively mechanical steps, it must not go on until it becomes mindless and boring. Always consider what you aim to achieve by using drills and find out which types work best with your students. Only the meaningful is memorable. So, the sooner practice connects with communication and personal interests, the better. In fact, we should note that perhaps the best practice activities do not contrast teacher control with learner freedom, but bring the two together (Stevick 1980). In this way, the teacher controls the form to be practised, while encouraging learners to say something true and meaningful about themselves. For example, a simple way of practising the present perfect in the humanistic tradition referred to above (under *Feelings*) might be to ask learners to provide true sentence fillers within this pattern.

My (Uncle Zoran) lives in (Krakow). I haven't seen (him) for (ten years).

Freer practice

Freer practice activities may still involve giving learners opportunities to practise particular target-language items, but these become more communicative. They may offer greater freedom in the choice of language use and they start to shift the focus towards fluency and meaning. One example might be Materials extract 2.3, designed to practise the use of gerunds and infinitives.

There comes a point, of course, when free practice becomes a communicative task that offers so much freedom that students no longer need to use the language item they were practising! This is potentially how practice links up with communication. This is also where it is critical that students understand the point of what they are being asked to do. They can either take this

f   Choose **five** of the topics below and tell your partner about them.

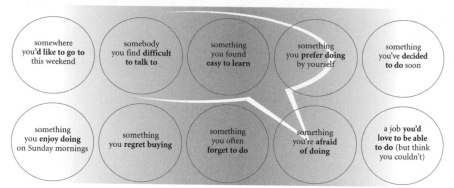

Materials extract 2.3   Oxenden and Latham-Koenig: New English File Intermediate, page 77

opportunity to use the target item to express their own meanings, or avoid it, or perhaps experiment with a combination of what they already know and what they are learning. As long as students are using the language in a meaningful way to communicate and are on-task, it should not be seen as a problem if they are not actually using the target form.

The *practice* element of ELT is related to conscious learning and accuracy. It is also connected with the idea of creating a structure within which students feel secure.

Strategies

Here are three ways of thinking about language learner strategies (based on Wenden and Rubin 1987):

1   Social strategies: learners can go to places where English is used.
2   Communication strategies: learners can practise phrases such as those below for entering a discussion:
I'd like to come in there…
Can I just make a point here?
3   Learning strategies: when learners come across a new word, they look out for opportunities to use it as soon and as often as possible in order to check if they are using it correctly.

The *strategies* element in ELT is related to the idea that learning can be improved if learners are more aware of what they are doing, how they are doing it, and what choices are available to them. Conscious learning will improve because of the new focus on how to learn. Subconscious learning will improve because of the extra involvement in what is going on.

Teaching strategies and raising awareness are also related to the idea of LEARNER AUTONOMY, or helping learners to achieve independence. Autonomous learners are aware of how they learn best; they set their own goals and objectives; and they organize their study to achieve them.

Many coursebooks contain activities variously called *learning to learn, learning strategies*, or *learner training*. They might include, for example, such activities as understanding dictionary entries, keeping vocabulary records, practice in deducing meaning from CONTEXT. The point of these activities is to make learners aware of how they learn and how they can take their learning forward without the presence of a teacher. In other words, how they can become autonomous learners.

In this connection, there is one important point to remember, however: in Chapter 1 we spoke of educational and cultural differences between learners. The concept of learner independence may be neither appropriate nor acceptable in some contexts and to some learners.

Moreover, in such contexts, if learners do not recognize what the teacher is doing as good teaching, they are unlikely to learn from it. You may, of course, decide that learner autonomy is nevertheless worth introducing, but you need to realize that you are not simply introducing a set of techniques, but also a set of cultural and ideological beliefs involving power, status, responsibility, and relationships.

Students may be persuaded, of course, but teaching has to respect the learners' starting point if they are to respect the teaching.

Summary

This chapter started by pointing out the multiple demands that learners face when communicating. It then introduced three levels of mental activity in language learning. It went on to describe two basic approaches to language teaching and related them to five key elements of the English language teaching tradition: *communication, feelings, rules, practice*, and *strategies*. It is helpful to focus on the different elements in order to understand them better, but it is also the teacher's job to weave all these strands together into a whole that is stronger than the sum of the parts.

Questions and activities

Think about your responses and then discuss them with a colleague if possible. Questions 1–3 all refer to Materials extracts 2.4–2.8 below.

1 Look at the activities in the materials extracts and say which of the five elements of ELT you think each one relates to most closely. What experience do you have of such activities, either as a learner or a teacher? What are your reactions to them?

2 Having established which element of ELT each activity mainly relates to, can you recognize other elements in any of the activities?

3 This chapter suggests that there are two broad approaches to language teaching. At which stage in each approach would you be likely to find the activities?

4 Look again at the characteristics of good learners in Chapter 1. How do they relate to the elements of ELT described in this chapter?

(For answers, thoughts, and comments on these questions, see page 183.)

STUDY SKILL Predicting content

Predicting the content of a text prepares you for what you are about to read. Being well-prepared helps comprehension.

Before you read a text:
■ look at the title   ■ look at any pictures

Use these to get an idea of what the text is about. Ask some questions (*Who? Where? Why?* etc.) to help you predict the content and to focus on the information you need.

Materials extract 2.4 Philpot: New Headway Academic Skills Level 2, page 17

---

16 Work with a partner. Make a list of the ten most important international events in your lifetime.

17 Choose one event. When did it happen, where were you, and what were you doing? Write notes like in exercise 4.

18 Tell other students in the class about it. Which story is the most interesting?

Materials extract 2.5 Hancock and McDonald: English Result Pre-Intermediate, page 63

---

b Complete with *a / an, the,* or – (= no article).

Can you give me __*a*__ lift to __*the*__ station? I want to catch __*the*__ 6.00 train.

1 We went to _____ cinema _____ last night. We saw _____ great film.

2 **A** Do you like _____ sport? **B** It depends. I hate _____ football. I think _____ footballers earn too much money.

3 He always wears _____ expensive clothes and drives _____ expensive car.

4 Jake's _____ musician and _____ artist.

5 They've changed _____ date of _____ meeting. It's _____ next Tuesday now.

6 We walked to _____ city centre but we got _____ taxi back to _____ hotel.

Materials extract 2.6 Oxenden and Latham-Koenig: New English File Intermediate, page 139

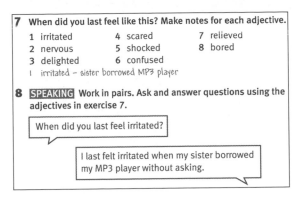

Materials extract 2.7 *Falla, Davies, Gryca, and Sobierska: Matura Solutions Intermediate, page 14*

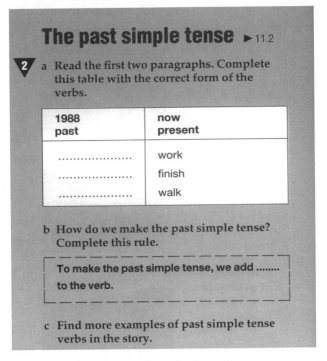

Materials extract 2.8 *Hutchinson: New Hotline Plus Starter, page 80*

3   THE ENGLISH LANGUAGE

If you look into any classroom, you can expect to see learners and a teacher working. These are the common elements we have considered so far: the people and the processes. It is now time to look more closely at the particular focus of the ELT class, that is, the language itself. We begin with the position of English in the world and the relevance of that position to ELT. We then look at various ways of thinking about what language is, as well as ways of teaching the different aspects of language.

English and 'Englishes'

English is the global language of the present historical period, serving for many people as the point of entry into the worlds of higher education, science, international trade, politics, tourism, and so on. At the same time, for many times more people, English creates a barrier between themselves and their fields of interest. Many people in their own countries will not be able to become doctors, for example, if they do not know enough English.

For reasons such as this, it is a mistake to contrast 'the ELT classroom' with 'the real world'. The ELT classroom is as real a part of the world as any other. As an English language teacher, you can see yourself as helping people develop their lives, or you can see yourself as supporting a system of world domination, or both. You can also ignore the issue for most of the time, but do not be surprised if it re-emerges now and again.

The role of English is a very broad issue, which can best be dealt with briefly here in terms of *ownership*, *attitude*, and *ability*.

Ownership

It is easy to think of English as belonging to countries such as Australia, Britain, Canada, New Zealand, the USA, and others, where the majority of the population is made up of mostly monolingual speakers of English who acquired the language as their mother tongue. It is from this position that the idea of the 'native speaker', to whom the language 'belongs', is derived. It is unhelpful, however, to confuse national languages with the concept of an international language.

Both authors of this book, for example, are native speakers of British English, but we are clearly not native speakers of English as an international language. The idea of a native speaker of this kind of English is a logical contradiction. An international language belongs to its users, not to the countries whose national languages have become internationalized. If a language belongs to its users, then it also becomes clear that:

- The important issue is not one of native/non-native speaker as an accident of birth, but of ability to use the language internationally.
- Native speakers of national Englishes (British, US American, etc.) are only partners in the international language. They also have to learn communication strategies if they are to use it effectively.
- People who learn to communicate in an international language are claiming something which is a part of their natural inheritance.

Another important consideration is the role of English in countries such as India, Malaysia, Nigeria, or Singapore, where established varieties of English are used in at least some aspects of public life: commercial, legal, or educational, for example. These varieties have national and regional significance outweighing that of British or US American varieties. It is for such reasons that, along with the concept of English as a global lingua franca, there is a great deal of discussion of the need to talk less about English, and more about 'Englishes'.

Given the importance of regional Englishes, the need for all users of English internationally to learn to communicate flexibly, and the established power of some Englishes (for example, British English and US American) in the fields of education and science, which English should we teach? There is no easy, or general answer to this question. In principle, a good teacher needs to be aware that there are different varieties of English in the world and to be sensitive to the needs of his or her learners in their particular sociolinguistic situation. It may often be the case that this decision is not yours to make, but you may still want to be clear that someone is making that decision and you may still want to have your own informed opinion on it.

Attitude

If people have a positive attitude towards a language and the speakers of that language, this will help them to learn it. In some cases, people might even be learning English because they want to be accepted into an English-speaking society and are driven by this integrative motivation.

Many people, however, learn English because they have a personal goal that has nothing to do with integration. This might be the case, for example, for German engineers on a project in Brazil and Argentina, where English will be the lingua franca at work. Their motivation would certainly be instrumental, in the sense that they would want English as a tool to help them achieve their professional purposes. Positive attitudes remain important, but now they need to have a positive attitude towards other people who have learned English and use it in the same way that they do, rather than towards those who speak it as a mother tongue.

As English spreads through continuing globalization, we might expect some version of the expression Teaching English as a Lingua Franca (TELF) to be used increasingly to express a sense of international and multicultural belonging in the language.

Ability

The term 'ability' implies a capacity to do something beyond just using the language itself. This something might be to pass an examination, to get a job, or to fit in with a new group of people. Acceptable standards of correctness, fluency, and appropriacy will always be involved in these activities, so teachers have a responsibility to help their students meet those standards. Because people have different expectations in different situations and may have to communicate with others whose expectations are different again, flexibility in communication is also something that needs to be taught and learnt.

These issues of ownership, attitude, and ability are especially important in the world of ELT today for two reasons. First, because most communication in English in the world takes place between people who both speak a different first language. Second, because the great majority of English language teachers have themselves learnt English as a second or foreign language. Given an appropriate level of ability, these teachers are the best possible models for their learners.

In the final analysis, you will inevitably teach your own English, whatever that may be. But analysing your attitudes about ownership and ability might help you see where your English fits in with English and Englishes in the world today.

Aspects of English

In order to say something, it is necessary to know the *lexis*, that is to say the words that express meanings, and also to know how to put those words together in *grammar* so that they make sense. We want to be sure that the *function* of what we are saying is appropriate in our *discourse*, that is, to our interactive communication with other people. We also need to know about the sounds of the language, or the phonology, so that our *pronunciation* is clear.

So, the headings here will be: *Lexis, Grammar, Functions, Discourse,* and *Pronunciation.* As each of these is discussed in turn, think about how they relate to the five elements of *communication, feelings, rules, practice,* and *strategies* discussed in Chapter 2.

Lexis

Knowing a large number of words and phrases in a foreign language is very important for learners to better their chance of understanding or making themselves understood. For ELT purposes, there are three important issues:

1 How to teach students new words
2 How to teach students what to do when they do not know a word
3 What to teach students about words

How to teach students new words

The more senses are involved in learning a word, the more likely it is that it will be remembered. So, if you are told the name of a fruit in a foreign language just as you have bitten into it, and are holding and looking at it, tasting and smelling it, you have a very good chance of remembering its name. Objects and pictures are widely used in language teaching for this reason. When you are teaching, think how you might use all the senses.

Words can be grouped according to what they refer to. Working with these lexical sets can help students to learn new words. Materials extract 3.1 is an example of an exercise based on lexical sets.

VOCABULARY

a Word groups. Underline the word that is different. Say why.

1	coin	cheque	bank	note
2	save	waste	mortgage	owe
3	exhausted	terrified	hungry	furious
4	delicious	wonderful	great	awful
5	flight	journey	trip	travel
6	coach	van	helmet	lorry
7	cycle lane	railway station	speed limit	traffic jam

Materials extract 3.1 Oxenden and Latham-Koenig: New English File Intermediate, page 34

Choose TOPICS to work on that relate to students' outside interests. This is not only motivating in a general way, it is surprising how broad a vocabulary some otherwise weak students have in their own areas of interest. Working

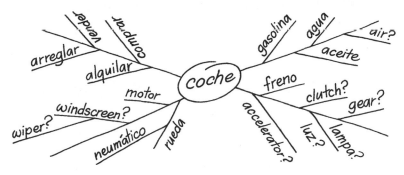

Figure 3.1 Word web

in an area of interest leads people to want to express their thoughts, and that generates a need to learn.

Students can help develop their own lexical sets by exploring their own associations. You can try this for yourself by developing your own mind map or word map in a foreign language.

Where you do not know the foreign language word, write the word in your own language. As a serious learner, you could go on to look up the word and write it in the target language. Figure 3.1 is our attempt in Spanish, beginning from the central word, *coche* (car).

Students should be encouraged to ask the teacher and each other for words when they want to express themselves. They should also keep their own vocabulary notebooks in which they note down:

● words or expressions that they hear or see and want to remember
● English words that they meet and simply do not understand
● words in their own language which they wanted to use but did not know the English for.

In these last two cases, they can ask or look them up later and write in the meanings.

Materials extract 3.2 is an example of an entry in a vocabulary notebook.

> hectic (adj) /ˈhektɪk/ = very busy
>   I had a hectic day at the office.

Materials extract 3.2 Soars and Soars: New Headway Plus Intermediate, page 13

Many learners find word cards useful. On one side they write the word they want to learn; on the other side, a translation, definition, or example illustrating the meaning.

---

ratty   In a <u>bad</u> mood:
          'OK, don't get ratty with me! It's not my fault!'

The more aware learners become of possible strategies, the more chance they have of discovering something helpful to themselves.

How to teach students what to do when they do not know a word

Students often stop reading or listening because they meet an unfamiliar word, or they give up trying to express themselves because they cannot think of the exact word they want.

As far as reading and listening are concerned, here are some useful approaches to teaching unknown words:

1 Encourage students to ignore them and carry on. Most probably the meaning will become clear, or it was not important.
2 Later, if students still want to know what a word means, they can try to work out the meaning. They can use clues:

- from their own language: is there a word with a common root (a COGNATE)? However, there can be problems with this strategy: the German *nervös*, for example, is often much closer in meaning to the English word *irritable* than to *nervous*. In other words, it is a false friend. Nevertheless, guessing a meaning based on the recognition of a cognate is more likely to be a help than a hindrance.
- from the structure of the word: is it like another English word? If students know the word *rely*, they can guess the meanings of *reliable* and *reliability*. As they recognize the significance of the SUFFIXES such as *-able* and *-ity* in making adjectives and nouns, they can also transfer this knowledge in working out the meanings of other words.
- from the context: it is often possible to guess the meaning of a word from the meaning of the words around it. For example, in a sentence like *The recognition of a cognate is more likely to be a help than a hindrance*, students may not know the word *hindrance*. However, structurally, they can see that it is a noun (it is preceded by an indefinite article and ends in *-ance*) and from the context, they can see that it is used in contrast to *help*. From this information they should be able to work out that *hindrance* means something like the opposite of *help*, something that obstructs you, gets in your way, or simply does *not* help.

3 Even from the most elementary level, students should be taught to ask, *What does ... mean?*

4 Teaching students to use a dictionary is an important part of the job. The more advanced they are, the more benefit they can get from a monolingual learner's dictionary. These contain a lot of information about the language and can be a very useful resource for independent study. It is important to remember that some students might not have learnt dictionary skills in their first language; that not all languages are alphabetical; and that among those that are, there are alphabets other than the roman. Good monolingual dictionaries have an introduction that explains to students how to use the dictionary, and teachers can help by taking their students through this information. Many dictionary publishers also have websites with reference materials, RESOURCES for teachers, and exercises to help students use the dictionary.

As far as speaking and writing are concerned, it is important for students to be able to ask for words in English. Expressions such as *What's the English for ...?* or *How do you say ... in English?* should be taught right from the beginning.

It is also important to develop the ability to say what you want to in another way, using CIRCUMLOCUTION. Three useful expressions to teach early on are:

- *you know:* a phrase for filling a pause and signalling that you want your listener to cooperate. (See examples below.)
- *a thing (for):* useful for avoiding unknown nouns, for example, *Have you got, you know, a thing for lifting a car?*
- *when you:* good for avoiding unknown verbs, for example, *I want to – you know, when you put the eggs in hot oil ...*

Note that we set out to consider how to teach words, but a great deal of the discussion has been about how to learn words. Much of the teacher's work is done by raising the learners' awareness of how to learn.

What to teach students about words

Building up a large vocabulary is an important part of language learning. If students are motivated to memorize lists of words by their experience of their own educational culture, it is difficult to see how this can do any harm. However, what we also know from experience is that *only* learning a list of words out of context is unlikely to get learners very far.

They also need to know how words are formed, how they can be combined, and how they are used together. We pointed out on page 36 that it can be helpful for learners to know how AFFIXATION works. In other words, how we can change either the meaning or the part of speech of a word (or both) by adding an affix to it. Knowing about relationships between words, such as synonymy, antonymy and hyponymy, can also be useful in organizing and learning vocabulary.

So far we have used 'word' and 'lexis' almost interchangeably. In fact, however, while *walk, walks, walking,* and *walked* might be considered four different words, they would be just one entry, or headword, in a dictionary and actually represent one lexical item, each one carrying different grammatical information. So it can be helpful to make the distinction between *word* and *lexical item*. Also, we have treated lexis as being concerned with mostly single words, but words are also used in combinations that may be more or less fixed. For example, nouns, verbs, adjectives, adverbs, and prepositions can be put together to form compounds, so *shop assistant* is a compound noun, while *bright red* is a compound adjective.

Idioms are fixed expressions where words are combined and take on a different meaning to the meanings of the individual words. For example, *she was over the moon when she got the job* means *she was very happy.*

Words also combine in collocations, that is, words that are frequently used together. For example, in English we *tell a story* rather than * *say a story*, and we might call something *brand new*, but this sense of *brand* does not occur with any other adjective.

Examples of authentic and natural language can be stored on a computer to build up a collection called a corpus. Corpora (the usual plural form of corpus) can help a great deal in learning about lexis. A computer can search for a particular word in a corpus and print out a list of all its occurrences, along with a stipulated number of words before and after the searched word in order to give a minimal context. Such a list of words in immediate context is called a *concordance*.

Below is part of a concordance from the British National Corpus (BNC) for the word *happy*. But before you look at it, think about the following question:

We can say 'happy about' something and we can say 'happy with' something. What's the difference?'

Courts are not always	**happy**	about deciding what vaguely-worded public duties
she that she, Matey, was not very	**happy**	about the idea that Mrs Darrell might become Mrs
Masklin felt less than	**happy**	about this.
was seeing her, because, I wasn't	**happy**	about the publicity, the way it had described audio
The Hearts manager is	**happy**	with the quality of players coming through the

Yes, we weren't too	**happy**	with the point situation because we considered it
second game, pronounced herself	**happy**	with her performance
renewable, if both companies are	**happy**	with the way it works.
who use peat-free composts are	**happy**	with the results, a survey by the Royal Society for

Examples taken from the British National Corpus

From the examples above, it would seem that, while there is no absolute rule, *happy about* mainly occurs in negative statements, whereas *happy with* tends to be positive. This is not a piece of information that would necessarily occur to someone simply by thinking about the collocation. That is the attraction of concordances, they give fresh insights into language as well as confirming established usage.

Lexis is a very complex business – knowing a word means knowing far more than just its spelling and translation. Furthermore, once we focus on patterns of words, the distinction between lexis and grammar is not nearly so clear-cut.

For example, there is a pattern that allows the speaker to say how important it is that something should happen:

It is	+	**adjective of importance**	+	**infinitive**
It is		important essential vital		to consider their future

But notice that if one wants to say how *likely* something is to happen, that pattern does not work anymore, and there are grammatical consequences:

It is	+	**adjective of probability**	+	**that**	+	**clause**
It is		likely probable on the cards		that		their future will be considered

So language can also be seen as collections of lexical items and lexical chunks that fit together in particular ways, where it is the choice among lexical options that determines what happens next. For this reason, it is becoming increasingly common to talk about lexico-grammar, rather than just lexis and grammar as two separate issues.

To take another example, it is also possible to focus on the meaning of lexical items that have for many years been treated as a part of grammatical structures, or sentence patterns. Thus, one common sentence pattern often taught in ELT is the one known as 'the second conditional':

If I knew her address, I would write to her.

While there is no obvious need to stop teaching this useful sentence pattern, it is also the case that there are other, related uses of *would* that might be taught at the same time, or subsequently. Learners could then become aware that the 'second conditional' is not a unique phenomenon, but part of a wider usage of *would*, involving meanings related to the imagined or hypothetical. For example:

- How much would it cost and can I have it delivered?
- A big pay rise would run the risk of stoking inflation.
- Ninety per cent of men would always keep money they found on the street.

As time passes, there is likely to be more work done along lexico-grammatical lines, and more work on making such observations available and useful for language teaching purposes. Do not be put off by new terminology, or by possible unfamiliarity with the complexities of such patterns. People use the patterns unconsciously. The process of becoming aware of them is one element of being a teacher. It can be seen as another aspect of moving from *experience* to *knowledge*.

For some learners, too, awareness-raising work on how language functions can be motivating. What is certain is that such developments will move hand-in-hand with the increasing use of computers in language teaching, not as exotic extras, but as a regular part of the way teachers work. We say more about this in Chapter 5.

Grammar

There is no single completely satisfactory way of describing the grammar of any language. This fact cannot, however, be taken as an excuse for not informing oneself about the generally accepted basics of linguistic knowledge, or for not striving to learn more. Grammatical terms, such as *noun*, *verb*, etc. are used because they help us talk about the language as we try to understand and help others to understand how it works. Different grammar books may use different words to describe the parts of speech; one possible set is: *adjective, adverb, determiner, conjunction, noun, pronoun, preposition, verb*. It is important not only to know these grammatical terms, but also to be able to explain what they mean. How would you explain these terms to your students? If you are not sure, you could first look them up in your grammar reference book and then think how you might simplify and exemplify what you find there to suit your learners.

This mixture of knowledge and ability to explain is something that you can build up as you work, and it is well worth the effort involved. A good pedagogic grammar book can be one of the most useful reference resources you have; you will find some suggestions in the Sources and Further Reading section. (See page 195.)

Just as grammatical terms help us to discuss the language and understand it, teachers usually make grammatical generalizations as and when they seem useful to learners. Students might be told *Don't use an infinitive after 'suggest'* because the teacher knows that * *Michael suggested to leave the party* is a common error.

Students might also be told *Use 'some' in positive sentences and 'any' in negative sentences and questions* because that generalization will help them with a lot of the straightforward utterances that they are likely to use at an early stage. But students need to understand that they can make better rules as they learn more, and teachers need to know enough grammar to be able to respond satisfactorily when a student asks about sentences such as *Do you want some coffee?* and *Please take any of them.* It is important to make it clear when making generalizations that these are not absolute rules, so that learners do not lose faith in what their teacher tells them ('But you said that...!').

If you grew up with English as your L1, you may never have studied the grammar and lexis of the language. As an English language teacher, however, such knowledge is essential. Without good grammatical aware-ness, you may be able to avoid awkward situations on the basis of your fluency and insight, but you will not be in a position to give your students the help they need.

If you have learnt English as a foreign language yourself, you probably have a good grasp of the basics of English grammar and lexis, as well as an insight into what your learners may find difficult. Nevertheless, you may not be able to answer all the questions you are asked. So, there are two things just as important for a teacher as having a sound knowledge of grammar:

1 You have to be able to admit that you do not know something.
2 You have to be able to find the answer.

If you grew up using English, it is relatively easy to say, *I don't know, I'll look it up for you.* (Then you have to make sure that you do so, and explain what you find to your students. And as they advance, it is worth spending time showing them how they can look things up for themselves.)

If you have learnt English as a foreign or second language, it may be more difficult to say *I don't know*, because it may undermine your confidence, you may worry about what your students will think and, in some cultures, you may also be seen as losing face. But since *nobody* knows the whole of a grammar, you really have to decide for yourself whether you are going to base your confidence on:

• a pretence of knowing, or
• discouraging students from asking questions, or
• an ability to look things up and explain.

Teaching the grammar of the language takes up a great deal of ELT time, particularly in the early stages, and we shall return to the topic at some length in Chapters 7 and 8. Before concluding this section, however, it is worth returning to the five elements of the ELT tradition (*communication, feelings, rules, practice,* and *strategies*) and relating them to grammar teaching. The importance of rules and practice should be obvious; learning how to use a grammar book is an important strategy already mentioned.

Remember also the importance of communication and personal feelings in ELT when teaching grammar. Here is a simple scenario to practise the past simple, contrasting it with the present perfect, while at the same time activating the potential for expression of authentic human emotions:

1   The teacher writes on the board a list of adjectives such as *frightened, surprised, overjoyed, angry, delighted, relieved.*
2   Students work in pairs.
3   Student A chooses an adjective and asks: *Have you ever felt really …?*
4   Student B thinks about it and replies: *Yes, I have/No, I haven't.*
5   If the answer is *No,* Student A asks again with a different adjective.
6   If the answer is *Yes,* Student A asks: *What happened?*
7   Student B describes the incident.
8   The students change roles.
9   The teacher could follow this up with Question 3 at the end of this chapter.

Functions

In the discussion of communication in Chapter 2, we talked about the importance of:

- getting a message across
- getting things done.

The idea of teaching functions in ELT has emerged from the second of these concerns. When people say something, they also do something; when they use grammatical structures, they also carry out language functions. Here are some examples to make this clear:

Saying this		Doing this
I'm sorry but I can't come.	usually means	Declining an invitation
I think they'll lose.		Predicting
You must take that book back.		Expressing obligation
When will they deliver the new chairs?		Enquiring
Turn all the lights off before you leave.		Instructing

Unfortunately, there is no simple way of relating functions to each other, nor of relating them to grammatical structures, as there is no one-to-one correspondence between form and meaning. The same function can be realized by different FUNCTIONAL EXPONENTS while the same grammatical structure can be used to express different functions, as the following examples show:

1   Can you reach that book?
2   Would you mind passing me that book?

Can you reach that book? could be a question about ability, in a context where someone is concerned that they have placed a bookshelf too high to be of use to another person, while both *Can you reach that book?* and *Would you mind passing me that book?* could be used to make a request. The context should make it clear which function is being expressed, while the choice of which form to use to make the request will depend on considerations such as who is being asked and what their relationship is to the speaker.

The use of functions in ELT is helpful in the following ways:

1   From the students' point of view, it is motivating to learn to *do* things in a language rather than just learning structures. It is also more immediately useful to them, especially if they are able to practise the expressions they have learnt, outside the classroom.
2   The teacher can use a function in order to CONTEXTUALIZE the teaching of a pattern. For example, you might encourage the use of student imagination and humour by inviting them to use the pattern *if + present simple, will + base form of the verb*, in the context of the function *threaten*:

- Think of ten different ways of completing the final sentence below. There will be a prize for the funniest.
- You are sitting in the cinema and the man behind you keeps tapping your seat with his foot. Twice you ask him to stop. Twice he starts again. You turn round and say, 'Look, if you do that again, I'll . . .'. This is particularly useful for students who have previously been taught in a straightforward structural fashion, because old ground can be covered and experienced in a new way.

3   Concentrating on functions provides an opportunity to deal with the sensitive matter of appropriacy, mentioned in Chapter 2. All the following ways of 'inviting' are correct, and all might be said fluently, but they are not neutral. The important thing is to choose the appropriate REGISTER or level of formality/informality for the person you are talking to and the context you find yourself in:

- Do you fancy dinner on Saturday?
- Could I invite you to dinner on Saturday?
- I was wondering if you might be free for dinner on Saturday?

Materials extract 3.3 is an exercise which teaches this kind of point:

> **Practically speaking** | Avoiding saying 'no'
>
> **1** Sometimes when we're asked a favour, we don't like to say 'no' in a direct way.
> Discuss questions 1–3 with a partner.
>
> 1 How easy is it for you to say 'no' when someone asks a favour?
> 2 Is it easier to say 'no' to some people than to others and in different situations? Why?
> 3 Which of the *Useful phrases* on page 135 could you use to avoid saying 'no' in a direct
> way to these favours?
> a 'Could you do the on-call shift next weekend?'
> b 'Could you help me look into this customer complaint we've received?'
>
> **2** Work with a partner. Take turns to respond to these favours. Refer to the *Useful
> phrases* on page 135.
>
> 1 'Do you think you could have a look at the results from our customer survey and
> prepare a report for the team meeting on Monday?'
> 2 'I'm supposed to be making a presentation at the investor relations meeting next
> Friday but I want to take a day's leave. Could you stand in for me?'
> 3 'Could you stay late tonight and help with the stocktaking?'
> 4 'We need someone to help at the conference next weekend. Are you free?'

*Materials extract 3.3 Duckworth and Turner: Business Result
Upper-Intermediate, page 63*

4 If a group of students is learning English for a particular purpose, whether
occupational (they are all waiters), or academic (they are all students of
chemistry), the teacher can make a list of things that they need to be able
to do with the language. This type of approach, called English for Specific
Purposes (ESP), has become a major component of ELT worldwide.

Discourse

Discourse means language in use, the way people use both written and spoken
language to communicate. Much of what we said about communication in
Chapter 2, and about functions in this chapter is relevant here. The two most
important aspects of language dealt with under this heading are:

- How do people use language to interact with each other?
- How is language organized beyond the grammar of the sentence?

Materials extract 3.4 is an activity aimed at practising structured interaction
according to a framework of how a discourse might develop.

With regard to discourse organization, while it is true that the rules of
grammar extend only to the structure of sentences, language in use is regularly organized beyond those boundaries. Sentences are joined together in
different ways. For example, they are linked by the use of pronouns, by logical
relationships, and by word repetition.

Let us look more closely at those last two sentences:

> Sentences are joined together in different ways. They are, for example, linked by
> the use of pronouns, by logical relationships, and by the repetition of words.

10   Work with a partner to make a dialogue. Person A: you are the host. You are dropping B off at his/her hotel. Person B: you are the visitor.

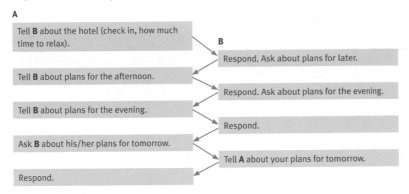

Materials extract 3.4   Gore and Smith: English for Socializing, page 12

The expression 'different ways' in the first sentence signals to the reader that at least two of these 'ways' are about to be listed. The expression 'for example' in the second sentence confirms the relationship of statement–example which organizes this tiny discourse of two sentences. The pronoun 'they' in the second sentence refers back to 'sentences' in the first. The words 'joined together' are repeated in the form of the paraphrase 'linked'. The repeated preposition 'by' signals the different 'ways' that are listed. These are all examples of what is called textual COHESION.

There is a lot more to texts than this, however. Certainly, learners do need to know how language is put together in sentences, and sentences organized into a text – what is called a bottom-up approach. In addition, however, they also need to be able to see a text as a whole and understand how it works – and this is called a top-down approach.

Texts vary according to the different purposes for which they are produced. A letter of complaint, for example, looks very different from a guidebook – they belong to different genres. For a start, the layout of the text will be different. Visual clues will often help learners to recognize immediately what type of text they are dealing with, and whether it is a page from a newspaper, or a letter, for example.

The text structure of different genres also varies. Scientific articles, for example, are often divided into sections such as: Introduction, Methods, Results, Discussion, Conclusion. If learners know to expect these different sections and to recognize them and the information they contain, this can help them to understand the content more easily.

Materials extract 3.5 shows examples of activities focused on the different discourse aspects of discursive essays. These activities help the students with the overall organization of the essay and with the language they need to link their ideas together.

WRITING Technology – good or bad?

1 Brainstorm arguments *for* and *against* mobile phones.
`Read Study Skill`

for	against
Can make a call at any time, anywhere.	Annoying in a public place e.g. in a restaurant.

<table>
<tr><td colspan="2">STUDY SKILL Organizing ideas (1)</td></tr>
<tr><td colspan="2">When writing an essay where you have to give two sides of an argument:
<ul>
<li>organize your ideas into arguments for and arguments against, and give some examples.</li>
<li>write a paragraph for, and a paragraph against, giving your ideas in a logical order.</li>
<li>write an introduction and a conclusion. Give your personal opinion in the conclusion.</li>
</ul></td></tr>
</table>

2 Read the essay. Did you have the same ideas?

Mobile phones

A Mobile phones are now part of our everyday lives. Most people find them essential and could not manage without them. However, there are also some drawbacks to owning and using a mobile phone.

B There are three main advantages to having mobile phones. Firstly, there is the convenience of being able to make or receive a phone call at any time and in any place. Secondly, they are essential for keeping in touch with family and friends. Parents worried about their children can always ring them to check they are safe, and children can let their family know if they are going to be late home. Finally, mobile phones can save lives. For example, if there is an accident, help can be called immediately, wherever the accident takes place.

C On the other hand, there are significant problems with the use of mobile phones. In the first place, using mobile phones can cause accidents, for instance, when people are driving and using their phone at the same time. In addition, the loud use of mobile phones in public places such as restaurants and cinemas is rude and can be very irritating for other people. Lastly, there has been an increase in street crime directly related to mobile phones. People have been attacked and their phones stolen from them.

D In conclusion, I believe that, despite the disadvantages, mobile phones are essential to modern life and that the advantages to owning one are far greater than the disadvantages.

3 Consider the purpose of each paragraph. Which paragraph A, B, C, or D… ?
- says why mobile phone use can be a good thing.
- introduces the subject.
- concludes and gives the writer's opinion.
- says why mobile phone use can be a bad thing.

4 `Read Study Skill` Go back through the essay. Underline 12 more linking words and phrases. Write them in the table.

sequence	firstly	
contrast	in spite of	
examples	e.g.	
endings	to conclude	

<table>
<tr><td colspan="2">STUDY SKILL Linking ideas (2)</td></tr>
<tr><td colspan="2">To help the reader understand your writing and follow your ideas, link short, simple ideas. Use:
<ul>
<li>firstly, secondly, …
for more than one argument or idea</li>
<li>however (see Study Skill p13), on the other hand, despite …
for a contrast between two ideas</li>
<li>for instance, for example, …
for an example to illustrate an idea</li>
<li>in conclusion, to sum up, …
for the final comment</li>
</ul></td></tr>
</table>

Materials extract 3.5   Philpot: Headway Academic Skills Level 2, page 24

Pronunciation

The three most important elements of pronunciation for ELT are:

1 *Stress:* which words or parts of a word, you say loudest and longest
2 *Intonation:* the way your voice goes up and/or down as you speak, especially at the end of what you say
3 *Phonemes:* as in the separate sounds of *pen:* /p/, /e/, /n/.

Stress

In dictionaries, WORD STRESS is usually marked with a small vertical line just above and before the stressed SYLLABLE, for example, 'record, re'cord.

Notice the grammatical difference that the stress makes here (noun→verb). It is certainly worth using exercises like those in Materials extract 3.6 to make sure that your students can actually hear different stress in words:

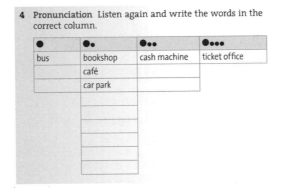

4 Pronunciation Listen again and write the words in the correct column.

●	●●	●●●	●●●●
bus	bookshop	cash machine	ticket office
	café		
	car park		

Materials extract 3.6 Hancock and McDonald: English Result Elementary, page 27

Sentence stress is important for two reasons. First, the RHYTHM of English speech tends to bounce along from stressed syllable to stressed syllable with the same amount of time between the stresses, no matter how many unstressed syllables intervene. If you say *This is a WONderfully eQUIPPED ROOM!* and tap out the rhythm of the stresses, you will find that the amount of time between *QUIPPED* and *ROOM* is the same as that between *WON* and *QUIPPED*, despite the syllables in between.

All this seems very natural to a person who has grown up speaking English, but it may not be so to the learner. In fact, this is a major reason why many people say that English speakers talk very quickly, or swallow their words, or mumble. The language teacher can help by providing a rhythm by tapping on the desk, or clapping hands, especially when students are practising a new language structure.

The second reason why stress is so vital is that L1 English speakers strongly emphasize words which they think are important to the meaning of what they want to say. Once again, as obvious as this may seem to people who have grown up using

English, not all languages work in this way. Try saying the following simple sentence in three different ways, each time with the main stress on a different part:

I'll help you.

What different situations come to mind as you say the sentence differently? What other changes take place in the rise and fall of your voice as you stress different words? As you can see, stress and intonation carry a lot of information.

Intonation

So intonation can change the meaning of what is said. Intonation is also closely related to politeness, and therefore to appropriacy. In normal speech outside the classroom, people will overlook grammatical inaccuracy and hesitancy, but if they feel that someone is being impolite, they are not so forgiving.

As with grammar, students do not want to learn about rules of stress and intonation for their own sake. They want to be able to use stress and intonation meaningfully. For this reason, the teacher has to keep them constantly in mind when teaching other things.

Even if the students are only repeating a dialogue, or practising new structures in a drill, or using functions in an exercise, the teacher should insist that they say their lines correctly, therefore meaningfully.

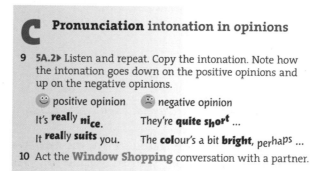

C **Pronunciation** intonation in opinions

9 **5A.2▶** Listen and repeat. Copy the intonation. Note how the intonation goes down on the positive opinions and up on the negative opinions.

☺ positive opinion   ☹ negative opinion

It's **really** ni_ce.   They're **quite** s_ho^rt ...

It **really suits** you.   The **colour's** a bit **bright**, per^haps ...

10 Act the **Window Shopping** conversation with a partner.

Materials extract 3.7 Hancock and McDonald: English Result
Pre-Intermediate, page 47

The teacher can also use feelings to help students in areas such as tone and pitch, where it is very difficult to state any rules, or even provide any clear descriptions of what is happening. There might be a specific pronunciation focus, such as there is in Materials extract 3.7.

Alternatively, a language practice exercise or drill, for instance, can be made both fun and useful when the students have completed it, by getting them to repeat the sentences with different emotions, for example:

TEACHER: Who can do number three again? This time say it as if you are surprised. Now say number eight as though you didn't mean it.

Many teachers, whether their first language is English or not, do not feel confident teaching intonation, or indeed other aspects of pronunciation. Fortunately, in most cases, coursebooks have exercises on features of pronunciation, with recordings as models. One really useful thing the teacher can do is to try out the exercises personally before going into class. The teacher's book associated with a coursebook often gives useful tips and advice. Alternatively, there are books available specifically on pronunciation. While you may not be able to use these in class, they can be a valuable source of information and development for you as a teacher.

Phonemes

Phonemes are the smallest separate sounds of a language that can make a difference in meaning. Where words are differentiated only by one meaningful sound, they form a minimal pair. If the phoneme /t/ is substituted for the phoneme /p/ in the word *pen*, the result is *ten*; if the phoneme /k/ is substituted for /f/, the word *phone* becomes *cone*.

Minimal pairs such as /b/ and /p/ in words like *bill* and *pill* differ only because /b/ is a voiced sound, i.e. it is pronounced with a vibration in the throat, whereas /p/ is unvoiced.

The way of writing sounds that we have used here is called phonemic transcription and it is always written between oblique lines /laɪk'ðɪs/. The attraction of the system is that there is one written symbol for each sound of spoken English, thus avoiding the complications of standard English spelling. Materials extract 3.8 is a PHONEMIC CHART showing the International Phonetic Alphabet (IPA) as it is used for standard British English and standard American English. Note that where two VOWELS are combined, such as in /eɪ/, these are called diphthongs.

For the teacher, a familiarity with this chart can be helpful in at least four ways:

1 It shows what separate sounds are involved in standard English. This kind of knowledge increases confidence.
2 You may discover that your own pronunciation differs from the standard in some places, as ours does. When you are challenged by students about a difference between your pronunciation and the pronunciation on a recording you have played, you can acknowledge this and explain exactly what the difference is, with reference to the IPA chart. In other words, differences between the teacher's English and standard English should not be a problem as long as you can show that you know what is going on.
3 Any good dictionary provides a pronunciation guide, using symbols similar to those in the chart below. This is important, because everyone meets words in their reading which they do not know how to pronounce.
4 While you might not know all the symbols by heart, the fact that you know how to use the IPA to demonstrate differences or check pronunciation gives you a skill you can feel confident about.

Consonants			
1	/p/	as in	**pen** /pen/
2	/b/	as in	**big** /bɪg/
3	/t/	as in	**tea** /tiː/
4	/d/	as in	**do** /duː/
5	/k/	as in	**cat** /kæt/
6	/g/	as in	**go** /gəʊ/
7	/f/	as in	**four** /fɔː/
8	/v/	as in	**very** /'veri/
9	/s/	as in	**son** /sʌn/
10	/z/	as in	**zoo** /zuː/
11	/l/	as in	**live** /lɪv/
12	/m/	as in	**my** /maɪ/
13	/n/	as in	**near** /nɪə/
14	/h/	as in	**happy** /'hæpi/
15	/r/	as in	**red** /red/
16	/j/	as in	**yes** /jes/
17	/w/	as in	**want** /wɒnt/
18	/θ/	as in	**thanks** /θæŋks/
19	/ð/	as in	**the** /ðə/
20	/ʃ/	as in	**she** /ʃiː/
21	/ʒ/	as in	**television** /'telɪvɪʒn/
22	/tʃ/	as in	**child** /tʃaɪld/
23	/dʒ/	as in	**German** /'dʒɜːmən/
24	/ŋ/	as in	**English** /'ɪŋglɪʃ/

Vowels			
25	/iː/	as in	**see** /siː/
26	/ɪ/	as in	**his** /hɪz/
27	/i/	as in	**twenty** /'twenti/
28	/e/	as in	**ten** /ten/
29	/æ/	as in	**stamp** /stæmp/
30	/ɑː/	as in	**father** /'fɑːðə/
31	/ɒ/	as in	**hot** /hɒt/
32	/ɔː/	as in	**morning** /'mɔːnɪŋ/
33	/ʊ/	as in	**football** /'fʊtbɔːl/
34	/uː/	as in	**you** /juː/
35	/ʌ/	as in	**sun** /sʌn/
36	/ɜː/	as in	**learn** /lɜːn/
37	/ə/	as in	**letter** /'letə/

Diphthongs (two vowels together)			
38	/eɪ/	as in	**name** /neɪm/
39	/əʊ/	as in	**no** /nəʊ/
40	/aɪ/	as in	**my** /maɪ/
41	/aʊ/	as in	**how** /haʊ/
42	/ɔɪ/	as in	**boy** /bɔɪ/
43	/ɪə/	as in	**hear** /hɪə/
44	/eə/	as in	**where** /weə/
45	/ʊə/	as in	**tour** /tʊə/

Materials extract 3.8 IPA Phonemic chart from Soars and Soars: New Headway Plus Intermediate, page 159

Teachers disagree about the usefulness of teaching the phonemic chart to language learners. Some people argue that students have enough problems without learning a strange new alphabet, and that teaching it is too academic for an ELT class. Others believe that learning this alphabet will help students to become independent learners, able to develop new skills based on their own increased awareness. Only you can know what will best suit your students, of course. But if you are interested in experimenting with using the IPA, here are two possible techniques you could use:

1   When you train your students to use a dictionary, it is worth spending time showing them how phonemic transcription works and giving them some practice in working out unfamiliar pronunciations. You can then respond to further inquiries as they arise, and students who want to develop this skill will have the chance to do so.

2   Problematic sounds in English for particular groups of students can be isolated. If your students confuse /iː/ and /ɪ/, so that the words *seat* and *sit* are pronounced identically, you could put these two symbols on the classroom wall with typical words under each one. When the mistake occurs

(at a time suitable for immediate correction), you simply point to one list or the other. After a while, the example words can be removed and just the symbols used.

Finally, we cannot leave the topic of individual sounds without noting the fact that they change when used in CONNECTED SPEECH, a feature of language that learners have to learn to deal with. A few examples will make the point clear.

CONSONANTS interact with each other. Take the three words, *an open book*. If they are all said separately, the final sound of the middle word will be /n/. But if they are said at normal speed in an utterance such as *There was an open book lying on the table*, what happens is that as the /n/ starts to form, the lips get pulled together for the following /b/ and the result is an /m/, something like: /əupəmˈbʊk/. Another example of connected speech is when a word ends in /t/ or /d/ and the next word begins with a consonant, the /t/ and /d/ sounds are often silent. So *mind the gap* becomes /maɪnðəˈgæp/ and *pleased to meet you* becomes /pliːztəˈmiːtʃuː/.

As far as vowels are concerned, perhaps the most important one is the sound called schwa, written /ə/. It is the sound we make at the end of the word *water*, /ˈwɔːtə/, or in the first syllable of the word, *forget*, /fəˈget/. It is very widespread throughout the language, and tends to be the sound that we move towards in unstressed syllables, reminding us that the three elements of *stress, intonation*, and *individual sounds* we identified earlier also interact with each other. This what we see in the shift from weak to strong forms of vowel sounds in sentences such as:

I can run **10** kilometres /kən/, with the main stress on '10', and
I **can** run 10 kilometres /kæn/ with the main stress on 'can'.

Vowel sounds can also disappear, along with the entire syllable. If we go back to our earlier example of *a wonderfully equipped room*, the word *wonderfully* in isolation has four syllables, but in actual speech it would more often be said and appear as three syllables: /ˈwʌndəfli/.

With reference to connected speech, it is worth noting that in all the examples we have given, we have used CONTRACTIONS, or contracted forms, such as *I've* instead of *I have*. It is important to introduce students to these right from the start, as they are a key feature of spoken English.

One last example is of something that seems to illustrate a language change, that is the replacement of /t/ in the middle and at the end of words by what is called a glottal stop, /ʔ/, so that the utterance *I've got a bottle of water*: /aɪvˈgɒtəˈbɒtələvˈwɔːtə/ sometimes contains no actual /t/ sound in the connected speech of an increasing number of the British population, sounding something like: /aɪvˈgɒʔəˈbɒʔələvˈwɔːʔə/

We would not necessarily teach this relatively new native speaker variety to students needing an international language, but if they were studying or living in Britain, they would need to be able to understand it.

Explanation cannot play a large part in teaching pronunciation. You can help your students to develop a 'good ear', partly by using models other than yourself, so that your students get used to a variety of pronunciations, but mostly by providing your students with a wide range of listening and practice activities. For example, when a student says something really well, you could use that student as a model and encourage everyone to listen carefully.

In everyday work, there are two points to keep in mind:

1 Make teaching pronunciation a constant element of the rest of your teaching. (See Materials extract 4.1 on page 58 for an example of how highlighting stress and connected speech can support communicative ability.)
2 Give short but regular bursts of treatment to aspects of pronunciation that seem particularly relevant to your students.

Summary

In this chapter we have considered the role of English in a variety of different contexts around the world. We have discussed ELT as an international activity that respects different models and aims to support global communication. We have also looked in some detail at what a language is made up of: *lexis*, which we *pronounce* and bring together in *grammar* and beyond it in order to *function* in our *discourse* with other people.

Questions and activities

Think about your responses and then discuss them with a colleague if possible.

1 Does English really belong to an international community? Or does it really belong to those people who grew up as native speakers of English? What points would you raise in this argument?
2 Do you have a favourite way of remembering words in a foreign language? Ask others and find at least one different strategy that you can try out.
3 What does your reference grammar tell you about sentence patterns? What does it say about the verb patterns:

- I stopped him hearing the news.
- I stopped him to hear the news.

How would you explain that difference?

4   While it is true that nobody can explain all the rules of English grammar, every-
    one can keep learning, and there is a basic minimum of grammatical knowledge
    teachers need to equip themselves with. The table below shows terms from the
    grammar section of the TKT glossary. If you are not sure what any of them refer
    to, check them in the TKT glossary or your reference grammar.

TKT grammar terms

Active voice	Infinitive	Present simple/continuous
Adjective	–ing/–ed adjective	Pronoun
Adverb	Intensifier	Proper noun
Auxiliary verb	Interrogative	Punctuation
Article	Irregular verb	Quantifier
Aspect	Main clause	Question tag
Base form of the verb	Modal verb	Reflexive pronoun
Clause	Noun	Regular verb
Collective noun	Object	Relative clause
Compound noun	Object pronoun	Relative pronoun
Conditional	Participle (past and	Reported statement
Conditional forms	present)	Reporting verb
Conjunction	Passive voice	Second conditional
Connector	Past perfect simple/	Singular noun
Countable noun	continuous	Subject
Demonstrative adjective	Past simple/continuous	Subject-verb agreement
Demonstrative pronoun	Personal pronoun	Subordinate clause
Dependent preposition	Phrase	Superlative adjective
Determiner	Plural noun	Tense
Direct question	Possessive adjective	Third conditional
Direct speech	Possessive pronoun	Third person
First conditional	Possessive 's'/whose	Time expression
Gerund, –ing form	Preposition	Uncountable noun
Grammatical structure	Present continuous for	Used to
Imperative	future	Verb/verb pattern
Indirect question	Present perfect simple/	
Indirect speech	continuous	

Table 3.1   TKT grammar terms

5   Make a list of all the language functions you carry out in one morning. Write
    down different ways of carrying out those functions in English or in any other
    language. What would lead you to choose one way rather than another?
6   Choose any short text. Can you see the ways in which the text is linked
    together, so that it is more than just a series of separate sentences?

There is no key for this chapter because all the questions above are reflective/prac-
tical and depend either on experience or the materials found by each teacher.

4 MATERIALS

As we said at the beginning of the last chapter, when you look into an ELT classroom, you expect to see learners and a teacher carrying out activities in English. What you will also expect to see are teaching materials, and they are the focus of this chapter. Let us begin with two fundamental points about materials:

1 It seems reasonable for a teacher to ask 'How do I teach these materials?' In one sense, that *is* a reasonable question, but only as long as the relationships between teachers, learners, and materials are clear. That is to say, the teacher's purpose is not to teach materials at all: the purpose is to teach the learners and the materials are there to serve that purpose. When there is a mismatch, there is no point in trying to fit the learners into the materials. It is the materials, or the use of them, that need to be changed.

2 At the same time, for as long as a teacher is using a certain set of materials, even if their appropriateness seems questionable, it is important to use them with enthusiasm. A negative attitude from the teacher towards the materials is strongly demotivating for the learners; it takes away their feelings of security and purpose.

In this chapter, we shall look at published materials, teacher-produced materials, student materials, and authentic materials.

Published materials

There is a vast range of published ELT material now available. Courses for general English come complete with student books and audio cassettes or CDs to use in class, a workbook or activity book for homework, and a teacher's book. Many also have a video cassette or DVD, a teacher's resource pack, a separate skills book, and a student audio cassette or CD.

Increasingly, coursebooks are sold with a student CD-ROM or DVD included. This usually contains extra practice and answers, in such areas as grammar, writing, listening, or vocabulary, as well as progress tests, so students can check how they are getting on.

More recently, some publishers have set up websites associated with a particular coursebook series. Generally, these offer students further practice, much in the same way as the CD-ROMs do, but there may also be links to other resources, such as online dictionaries. The websites also frequently help students with learning strategies such as keeping vocabulary notebooks. Sites like these will almost certainly be attractive to students, but they can also be unfocused or rather confusing. Students will need some guidance from the teacher, at least initially, in order to be able to use them effectively for self-study. (See Chapter 5 on the use of technology in language teaching.)

The most recent development is the availability of digital versions of some coursebooks. Digital coursebooks can be used on a variety of classroom equipment, such as the interactive whiteboard or the computer laboratory. We will return to this in Chapter 5.

In this section, we refer explicitly to printed coursebooks. Our comments also apply to the huge range of stand-alone books of SUPPLEMENTARY MATERIALS that focus mainly on particular types of classroom activity, or on the specific language SKILLS of reading, writing, speaking, and listening. (See Chapter 9).

Publishing ELT materials is big business, and it arouses strong feelings. Some teachers are as fiercely against coursebooks as others are in their favour. The pity of it is that some teachers on both sides of the argument simply follow books instead of using them. And some teachers devote massive amounts of time and energy into producing a poor quality, home-made version of what is already available. They are then often disappointed by the reaction of their students, who prefer the appeal and authority of a good coursebook.

We said earlier that teachers do not teach materials, they teach students and they use materials in the process. Certainly, some materials are better than others, but committed teachers can usually use just about any kind of published material, adapt it, and use their energy and creativity in areas where it is more needed. So it is important to develop a clear idea of what published materials can and cannot do, and what can be expected from them.

When you are given a published coursebook to use, you should be able to expect that a great deal of effort has gone into making it:

- *Reliable* in terms of the overall choice and sequencing of what is taught, the correctness of information, and the dependability of the exercises and activities. However, coursebooks are not infallible: mistakes creep in to any text; point this out to students in a positive way.

- *Attractive* in terms of topics, layout, and illustrations. You have to check this with students, of course. What is attractive in one context may not be in another.
- *User-friendly* in that at least one way of using the materials is clear to teacher and students, giving them a sense of security when it comes to doing class work and homework. Wherever possible, get a copy of the teacher's book, which will give you other options to consider when using the materials.

Let us look at the beginning of a typical coursebook unit, in Materials extract 4.1, in terms of the three criteria listed above.

Materials extract 4.1 is taken from an elementary level coursebook for adults. We have an attractive layout, with colourful visuals on one side of the page and activities on the other. The context is used to present prepositions of place and to practise useful expressions for giving directions, together with vocabulary related to common commercial buildings. Let us assume that this type of vocabulary and this area of language fit reasonably well into the learning progression of a book designed for this level and age of student. The student book also makes it clear how the material can be used. In this way, at a superficial level, at least, we have begun to use our criteria to assess the material on offer. This kind of approach becomes more important the more choices have to be made.

Choosing a coursebook

For teachers who are in a position to choose the book they will use, this is probably one of the most important decisions they will make. As we said above, if the teacher does not like the book, it is unlikely that the students will. Ultimately, it is only by actually using a coursebook with a particular group of learners that all its strengths and weaknesses become clear; but a principled and reasoned choice can still be made.

One way of choosing a coursebook is to start by trying to get a general overall impression of it. This is what Littlejohn (1998) calls the *impressionistic* method. Here are some questions that can be asked about the book:

1 Does the material seem appropriate to the age and level of the students?
2 Is the layout attractive? Will the students like it? Are the pages over-crowded? Are they boring to look at?
3 Is the book culturally appropriate for the students? For example, in Materials extract 4.1, the map would be meaningful for students in many countries, but for those in other countries it most certainly would not.
4 Does the balance of the four skills of listening, speaking, reading, and writing match the needs of the students?
5 How is the book organized? (The list of contents at the front of the book should provide a map of its organization.) Some teachers prefer a

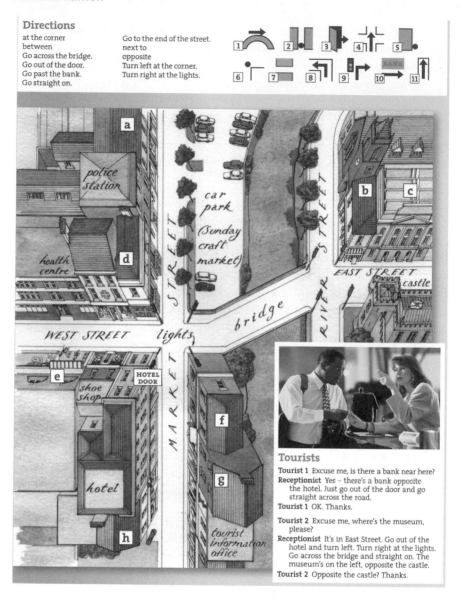

Directions

at the corner
between
Go across the bridge.
Go out of the door.
Go past the bank.
Go straight on.

Go to the end of the street.
next to
opposite
Turn left at the corner.
Turn right at the lights.

Tourists

Tourist 1 Excuse me, is there a bank near here?
Receptionist Yes – there's a bank opposite the hotel. Just go out of the door and go straight across the road.
Tourist 1 OK. Thanks.

Tourist 2 Excuse me, where's the museum, please?
Receptionist It's in East Street. Go out of the hotel and turn left. Turn right at the lights. Go across the bridge and straight on. The museum's on the left, opposite the castle.
Tourist 2 Opposite the castle? Thanks.

coursebook with a theme running through a unit because they feel that gives coherence to a lesson. But not all teachers feel that way.

The second step (Littlejohn, 1998) is to get a more in-depth view by, for example, choosing a unit at random and looking at it in detail. Here are some possible questions to ask:

1 Are the students likely to be interested in and engage with the materials?
2 Is there a good variety and balance of activity types?

How to give and follow directions

v places in town; directions　ᴘ linking words together

A　Vocabulary directions

1　Look at **Directions** opposite. Work with a partner. Match the phrases with pictures 1–11.
Example　at the corner = 6

2　9B.1▶ Listen and repeat.

3　Test a partner.
Example　**A** Picture 1?　**B** Go across the bridge.

B　Listen to directions

4　9B.2▶ Don't look at the page opposite. Listen to the conversations. Write *true* or *false*.
　1　The bank is next to the hotel.
　2　The museum is opposite the castle.

5　Listen again and read **Tourists** opposite. Find the bank and the museum on the map.

6　Say the conversations with a partner.

7　9B.3▶ The receptionist gives directions to these places. Listen and match the tourists with the places.

art gallery　bookshop　gift shop
~~post office~~　restaurant　supermarket

Tourist 3　*post office*
Tourist 4　_____

Tourist 5　_____
Tourist 6　_____
Tourist 7　_____

8　Listen again. Find the places in exercise 7 on the map.

9　Read the audio script on ≫ p.156 and check.

10　Where are the places? Write *true* or *false*.
　1　The post office is next to the tourist information office.
　2　The bank is between the gift shop and the tourist information office.
　3　There's a restaurant on the corner of River Street.
　4　The supermarket is next to the shoe shop.
　5　The museum is next to the restaurant.
　6　The bookshop is between the shoe shop and the health centre.

C　Pronunciation linking words together

11　9B.4▶ Listen and repeat. (The final letter of the first word sounds like it's the first letter of the second word: *left at* sounds like *lef tat* /'lef tət/.)

left‿at the corner /'lef tət ðə 'kɔːnə(r)/
out‿of the door /'aʊ təv ðə 'dɔː(r)/
right‿at the lights /'raɪ tət ðə 'laɪts/
straight‿across /'streɪ təˈkrɒs/
walk‿across /'wɔː kəˈkrɒs/
bank‿opposite /'bæŋ ˈkɒpəzɪt/
post‿office /'pəʊs tɒfɪs/
tourist‿information /'tɔːrɪs tɪnfəˈmeɪʃn/

12　Where one word ends with a consonant sound and the next word begins with a vowel sound, write ‿.
　1　Stop at the end of the street.
　2　Turn left at the lights and walk across the street.
　3　Walk across the bridge and stop opposite the castle.

13　9B.5▶ Listen and repeat the sentences.

D　Give directions

14　Write directions from the hotel to two places on the map.

15　Work with a partner. Read out your directions. Your partner finds the place on the map.
　Example　**A** Go out of the hotel and turn left. Turn left at the corner and it's on the left after the shoe shop.
　　　　B The supermarket?
　　　　A Yes, that's right.

ABCD　Put it all together

16　Work with a partner.
　Student A　Draw these on the map opposite.
　　　　an underground station　a café
　　　　a cash machine
　Student B　Draw these on the map opposite.
　　　　a bus stop　a newspaper kiosk　a phone box

17　Ask and give directions. You are at the hotel.
　Student A　You want to find a bus stop, a newspaper kiosk, and a phone box.
　Student B　You want to find an underground station, a café, and a cash machine.

　Example　**A** Excuse me, is there a bus stop near here?
　　　　B Yes, ...

Materials extract 4.1　Hancock and McDonald: English Result Elementary, 88–89

3　Are the language points explained in a way that suits the teacher's own view of language and language teaching and learning?

4　Is it possible to see how the material could be taught even without the teacher's book?

5　Does the material lend itself to a variety of ɪɴᴛᴇʀᴀᴄᴛɪᴏɴ ᴘᴀᴛᴛᴇʀɴs? (See Chapter 6 for examples.)

6　Is it possible to see how the material could be adapted to suit a particular group of learners?

It may seem contradictory to begin by thinking about how to change a book, but coursebooks are designed for large markets, not for specific groups of students. The teacher should always be looking for ways to bring the book closer to a particular group of learners. We will be returning to this theme below.

The teacher's book

A good teacher's book is a useful tool which should go well beyond simply giving the answers to the exercises in the coursebook. Before reading on, you might like to reflect on what you would find useful in a teacher's book at this stage in your career.

Here are some things that a good teacher's book should contain:

1 An explanation of the view of language on which the coursebook is based. For example, does it see language as a series of structures to be put together piece by piece? Or does it view language holistically, as a resource for communication?
2 An explanation of the approach to language learning and teaching on which the coursebook is based, the principles that underlie it, and indications as to how it can be put into practice.
3 The rationale that underlies the way the coursebook and the activities in it are organized.
4 A lesson plan for each unit, together with alternative ways of using the material and suggestions for supplementary activities.
5 An explanation of the purpose of each activity so that the teacher knows why a particular activity is being done and how it fits into the overall lesson AIMS.
6 Extra activities to choose from when students need more practice in a particular area.
7 Progress tests, so that the teacher and students can check how well they are keeping up with the course.

A good teacher's book can also be a very useful tool for professional development, especially for teachers at the start of their careers, or those who want to experiment with changing their approach in some way. Some teacher's books come with a DVD showing extracts from actual lessons, followed by the teacher's comments on the materials. In terms of professional development, this is a potentially very useful innovation in teachers' books.

Let us now look at what a published coursebook cannot provide:

• Insight into the interests and needs of *specific* students
• Decisions about which materials to use, and which to change, supplement, or leave out

These elements must, of course, be supplied by the teacher. This is just one of the areas where method and materials overlap. But first let us look at the role of teacher-produced materials.

Teacher produced materials

Teacher-produced materials can range from the odd activity used to supplement the coursebook to materials for a whole course. Let us look first at adapting published materials.

No matter how good the published materials, it is unlikely they can be used exactly as they are; the teacher will almost certainly need to adapt them in some way to suit a particular group of students and the aims of the lesson.

In somewhat more detail (see McGrath, 2002), materials might be adapted in order to:

- make the lesson more interesting/varied
- cater for different learning styles
- bring the materials closer to the local context
- make the materials more culturally appropriate
- bring the material more up to date
- vary classroom interaction patterns.

Adaptation can take various forms. Sections of a coursebook unit might be:

- missed out completely
- replaced with something different
- extended in some way
- modified in some way.

To exemplify these points, let us go back to the materials in 4.1. In teaching these materials, it is unlikely that the teacher would miss anything out completely, as all the activities are connected. However, if time were short, Exercise 9 could be dropped and teacher-to-class feedback used for the answers to Exercises 7 and 8. By the time the class got to Exercise 10, it could be that the teacher would prefer the students to start producing some of the expressions, so Exercise 10 could be replaced with something like this gap-fill activity:

Look at the map and complete the sentences below, using the words in the box below:
1 The supermarket is _____ the health centre.
2 The bank is _____ the gift shop.
3 There's a bookshop _____ Market Street.
4 The police station is _____ the bookshop and the art gallery.
5 The gift shop is _____ the hotel, _____ the bank, and the tourist information office.

| between | on the corner of | next to | opposite |

Alternatively, Exercise 10 could be done as it is in the book, but followed by the exercise above as an EXTENSION TASK to check understanding and/or to give further practice if the teacher feels either of these is necessary.

Another form of extension would be to exploit the potential the materials offer for activating and extending the learners' grammatical knowledge at a metacognitive level. The unit focuses on prepositions and prepositional phrases, so we might want to be sure that the learners notice these terms as they work. The teacher might ask:

> *Does anyone know any other prepositions we might use?*

Or

> *As you describe where the places are, use these prepositions or any others you know.*

Or, under appropriate circumstances:

> *What sort of words are these prepositions? What are they for? What do they do?*

So the same materials can be modified and extended in different ways and for different reasons, according the particular group of learners.

In most teaching situations, the most important role of teacher-produced materials is to bridge the gap between the classroom and the world outside. The teacher might therefore produce a map similar to the one in Materials extract 4.1 above, but which represents the students' local area or a well-known area of their city. The same activities can then be carried out in local terms, thus personalizing the students' learning. If the students need a lot of practice, the teacher-produced exercise can follow the one in the coursebook. If less practice is needed, the localized material might replace the exercise in the book. In either case, the result should be that:

- The use of English is related to the world outside the classroom.
- There is authentic communication between the learners.

Unless and until teachers become very skilled at materials production, with resources and facilities to back them up, perhaps the most useful thing teachers can do is to create this type of extension of given exercises to suit the students' situation, in a way that engages their imagination, intelligence, sense of humour, and interest.

Having said that, some teachers may find themselves teaching a course for which no suitable published materials exist. This is not uncommon in the area of English for Specific Purposes (ESP), where, as the name suggests, students have very specific needs. ESP coursebooks tend to be limited to the fields of medicine, science, and business (the biggest markets!). So in the case of, for example, English for agricultural science, or English for pharmacy, the teacher may be faced with a choice between adapting an existing ESP book or preparing his or her own materials, most usually by using authentic materials.

Authentic materials

The word *authentic* is used in different ways in ELT, but the most common use of the expression *authentic materials* refers to examples of language that were not originally produced for language learning purposes but which are now being used in that way. So, if you decide to cut an article out of a newspaper and use it in class, this would be an example of using authentic material. Authentic materials are most often reading texts, sometimes listening texts. You can create an even greater sense of authenticity of this type by bringing into class not just copies of authentic texts, but real objects (sometimes referred to as realia). Textual realia such as brochures, leaflets, menus, and timetables, etc. blur the boundaries between the classroom and authentic social contexts.

There are two reasons why authentic materials are so important:

1 *Language*. The ability to cope with authentic materials represents the actual goal of language learning, and such materials also often include the difficulties that learning materials tend to avoid. All learners need practice in meeting these real challenges. Even in the early stages, students should learn how to respond to language they do not fully understand.
2 *Motivation*. Authentic materials create a direct link with the world outside the classroom, bringing the *means* of learning and the *purpose* of learning closer together, thus increasing motivation.

One way to use authentic materials is to take the exercises and frameworks used with other materials and combine them with your own.

Here are two higher-level general exercises which work well with appropriate texts and which train students in the useful SKILLS of reading and listening:

1 As you read the text, put a tick (✓) in the margin if you agree with the writer and a cross (✗) if you disagree. Then discuss your ticks and crosses with a partner.
2 What problem is the speaker discussing? What solutions have been tried? What was wrong with them? What solution does the speaker suggest?

With careful choice of text and suitable activities, authentic texts can be used early on in language learning. To practise numbers, for example, you could record an international weather forecast and ask your students to listen for the predicted temperatures in different countries. This can be made even easier by giving students a list of names and numbers and asking them to link the ones they hear.

Introducing authentic materials in the early stages of learning has the advantage of presenting learners with the sort of language they will meet outside the classroom early on. It also means that they will get used to the idea that they do not need to understand every word in order to function communicatively in English. Getting learners past the immediate panic of 'It's all too much! I understand nothing!' is already a major achievement.

The concept of making materials local and authentic is also at the centre of what is meant by student materials.

Student materials

The examples of student materials given below are fairly typical of some published coursebooks. Some writers recognize that their books are only there to initiate the language learning process, which the teacher must then link with the lives of the students. Not all coursebooks are so helpful.

We can think of student materials in two ways:

1 learning materials produced by the students
2 the students themselves as materials.

Student-produced materials

Let us return to Materials extract 4.1. We have seen how the teacher can personalize the materials by using local maps. For the final activity (ABCD Put it all together), rather than using the map in the book, or producing a map yourself, you could ask your students to draw and label maps of their own neighbourhood or their own city. They can then use these to ask for and give directions, thus personalizing the materials even further.

To take another example, many coursebooks introduce *there is/there are* and prepositions of place by using pictures of rooms and asking students to describe where the furniture is or where various objects are. As a follow-up to such activities students can be asked to draw or to bring in photographs of their own rooms as the basis for an activity of the same type. The students are then using their own personal backgrounds to produce learning materials for their classmates. In addition to the effects noted under teacher-produced materials, the learners also have a *personal* investment in the materials, in that they have put something of themselves, their own background, knowledge, and creativity into the material and so have a personal interest in the outcome.

Students as materials

Coursebooks frequently use pictures of people as the basis for activities – to present vocabulary about clothes, for example, and to practise the use of the present continuous, as in *Sally's wearing jeans and a red jumper.* This activity gives everyone in the class a starting point, but the really useful work depends on what happens next. The classroom is full of real people wearing real clothes, and this can be used as the basis of extended practice. The teacher thus makes sure that students are learning words that are directly relevant to themselves and their lives. For example, the class might be wearing a variety of footwear (sandals, sneakers, trainers, and other types). It is not the textbook writer's business to know this; it is the teacher's business to make the connections. It is also the teacher's business to be sensitive to context and to learners' reactions – not all learners will be comfortable with having attention drawn to their clothes. It is exactly moments such as these that illustrate the difference between teaching the materials and taking responsibility for using the materials to teach learners.

When we see the learners as materials, we can also use our own methods to make learning enjoyable. We could, for instance:

- Ask a student to close his or her eyes and describe what someone else is wearing.
- Ask a student to describe what someone else is wearing until the rest of the class recognizes that person.
- Divide the class into pairs and ask each pair to do one of the above.

Similar activities can be devised around students' jobs, countries, interests – in fact, any aspect of their lives, providing, as we said in Chapter 2, this is handled sensitively by the teacher.

By using the students as materials, we can ensure that:

- the use of English is related to the world of the classroom
- there is authentic communication by and about the learners.

Students, of course, only work through a particular coursebook once (one hopes!), whereas teachers may use the same book with several classes in one year, or for several years running with different classes. So, relating the materials to the lives of the students is not only good for the learning process, it also introduces variety and freshness for the teacher.

The smaller your group of students, the easier it often becomes to encourage genuine PERSONALIZATION of the learning process.

For teachers working on a one-to-one basis, the learner's personal and professional environment becomes the content material, and teaching is then a kind of supportive pairwork which helps the learner live in that environment in English.

The Internet as a source of materials

The Internet can be an extraordinary resource for the language teacher, with huge potential for providing student-friendly material. The list of types of useful (general, not specific) sites is almost endless, but here are a few examples:

- Newspaper and TV sites are a useful source of up-to-date authentic material. Some of the most obvious sites are the BBC, CNN, the *Guardian*, and so on. But many English-language newspapers from countries where English is not the first language, such as the *Gulf News* in the United Arab Emirates also have websites. The advantage of these is that they have local news relevant to students. If you are not sure what is available in your country, there are many sites which list radio and TV stations, as well as newspapers in various countries.
- Some newspaper and magazine websites also have special sections for ELT. The *Guardian*, for example, has a TEFL site which provides useful links, as well as TEFL news.
- ELT publishers' websites not only give information about their materials but also contain a wealth of supplementary materials and even lesson plans.
- There are many dedicated ELT sites which outline lesson plans complete with materials. They also suggest ideas for tasks, warmers, and for teaching everything from a grammar point to speaking skills, and usually provide discussion forums or virtual 'staff rooms', which can be useful if you are teaching in relative isolation.
- There are a number of sites with video clips, which can be excellent for developing listening skills. (See Chapter 9.) *Videojug,* for example, has a series of short (2–5 minute) 'how to' clips with instructions on everything from making various dishes, to sewing clothes, to fixing things around the house. Eastman (2007) has many other suggestions.
- There are also many sites dealing with literature, tourist information, science, politics, and other areas of interest. The only limit is the teacher's creativity (and time!).

As with published materials, the starting points should always be the learners and the aims of the lesson, so the materials need to be chosen with that in mind. Unlike published materials, what you find on the Internet may not have been written by professionals and will almost certainly not have been researched and piloted. This is not to say that it will not be highly useable, but, like all materials, it should be considered critically and adopted with caution.

Summary

This chapter has explored what is available in terms of published materials in ELT and shown how these materials are often useful as a reliable basis for learning, but need to be adapted to suit local conditions. We have shown how teachers can create locally relevant materials from authentic texts and how students can produce their own materials and act as a source of materials themselves. Finally, we briefly touched on the Internet as an immensely valuable source of materials for both teachers and students.

Questions and activities

Think about your responses and then discuss them with a colleague if possible.

1 What is your experience of teaching or being taught a language from:
   - a coursebook?
   - teacher-produced materials?
   - student-produced materials?

2 Look at any coursebook or coursebooks you can find:
   - Are they attractive and user-friendly?
   - If you look at some sections in detail, do they seem reliable?
   - Do the books themselves help you localize the work they introduce?

3 Look at some material in a student's book and try to think of different ways of teaching it. Then check the teacher's book and see if it suggests any different ideas. Repeat this with different books. Try not to choose the best idea, but to see what each idea has to offer. They might all be useful in different circumstances.

4 Look at a variety of coursebook exercises and think about how you might:
   - produce material to relate the coursebook work to a particular class
   - get the students to produce a piece of related material
   - organize an activity to draw on the students' appearance, knowledge, or background as material
   - organize an activity in which the students really communicate with each other about themselves.

5 What is your experience of teaching or being taught a foreign language with authentic materials? Find an authentic text with which you could use one of the general exercises on page 63.

6 Look at one of the Internet sites listed on pages 201–202 that provides lesson plans. How useful do you think the site is? How much would you need to adapt the lesson plan to suit a particular class?

There is no key for this chapter because all the questions above are reflective/practical and depend either on experience or the materials found by each teacher.

5 ENVIRONMENT AND EQUIPMENT

Almost all classes take place in a room with furniture in it. This setting gives shape to the physical and psychological environment in which students and teachers work, and that is where we are going to start this chapter. We shall then look at the most basic piece of classroom equipment, the board. Finally, we shall make some brief comments on those items of teaching technology which can either help or hinder the teaching and learning process: the OVER-HEAD PROJECTOR (OHP), audio and video equipment, the computer, and the interactive whiteboard.

The classroom

Ideally, the classroom is a teaching space that is suitable for learning. This means, first of all, that it should be the right size and temperature and be well lit. It should also be clean and attractive, and have a shape that enables all the students to see the board and the teacher to see all the students. A cramped, cold, L-shaped room, with bare walls and little light is unlikely to encourage the development of the English-speaking community the teacher wants to create.

If the room is unsatisfactory in any of these ways, the basic question to ask is *Does it have to be like this?* You cannot change the size of a room, but you might ask the school or institution if another room is available. If all the classroom walls are bare, perhaps that is because no one ever asked if they could put up posters, or display student writing. It is always worth asking.

Perhaps teachers of other subjects do not want to work in a room with English language posters, charts, or articles from English language magazines on the walls. So might it be possible in future to timetable one room for English classes all the time or almost all the time?

Ensuring a safe, pleasant, and interesting environment to work in is a first step towards successful teaching. It is the teacher's responsibility to find out what can be changed and what cannot, and to make any changes without upsetting anyone. Once you have done what you can towards creating a suitable environment for your English-using community, you can concentrate on being positive about what you have.

Furniture

Furniture sends its own messages. Many living rooms are arranged so that all the seating faces the television – the message there is that the television monopolizes much of the time the families spend in their living rooms. Many classrooms are arranged so that all students face forward to the teacher – again, the message is clear:

- the teacher dominates
- all information will come from the teacher
- interaction between or among students is less valued.

Because the language class is concerned with communication and a variety of interactions, the arrangement of the furniture needs to send a different message. Figure 5.1 shows a good, general seating plan.

In the arrangement in Figure 5.1, everyone can look towards the front of the class when necessary, and everyone has a table to write on. If cooperative pairwork is needed, or if information needs to be shared by a pair, A and B can work together. If information needs to be divided between a pair, A and D can work together.

If group work is needed, A, B, C, and D can work together. All of this is possible without anyone having to move. The message then is that teacher and students are flexible, and will work and communicate with different people.

If the teacher wants the class to talk about a topic as a whole class, the tables can be moved out of the way, as in Figure 5.2. The message is that teacher and students are open to each other.

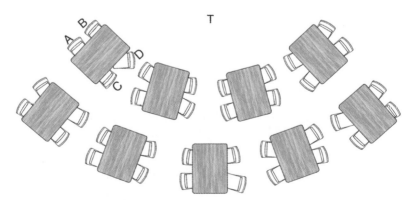

Figure 5.1 A general seating plan

Figure 5.2 A whole-class seating plan

It takes an effort to get students used to the idea of moving furniture, but with time it can be done efficiently; furthermore a little physical movement in class can be a natural and useful mini-break in concentration.

There may be pressure from colleagues and school cleaners to put the furniture back into neat rows after the class. It may be possible to ask cleaners to clean the room and leave the furniture where they find it. It may also be possible to tell colleagues that you will happily leave furniture the way the next teacher wants it, as long as the previous teacher leaves it the way you want it. If you are working in someone else's country, it is worth the effort to move the furniture back at the end of the class to the arrangement people think it 'should' be in. Whatever your response to the issue of seating arrangements, it is important to be politely assertive in your own way.

The fact that teachers, administrators, and school cleaners can react quite strongly to the way furniture looks in a room serves to underline the basic point that furniture is not neutral. If you do not use the furniture to conscious effect, it will quietly exercise its own effect.

In some classrooms, the furniture is fixed in place. The best way to get students into groups is often to have two turn round to work with the pair behind them, as in Figure 5.3, perhaps getting them to sit on the desk, if that is appropriate in the local context.

The ultimate message then is that the teacher and students need not be constrained into set positions, even if the furniture is. Each room sets its own challenge. You can ignore it, but you cannot make it go away.

One final point to underline is that the issues discussed above (arranging a room, moving furniture, dividing students into pairs and groups, and so on) involve the use of language. If you can make sure that the language used is

Figure 5.3 A group seating plan

English wherever possible, then you have already gone a long way to showing that English is not just a subject to be studied, it is a working means of communication. If you can establish that idea in the minds of their learners, you have already done an important part of the job. For some students, at least, it will then become attractive to try to integrate themselves into this small English-speaking community.

The board

In spite of the many technological advances in classrooms, the board is probably still the most common piece of equipment teachers use.

It is a good idea to spend a little time practising board writing. Like any kind of writing, this is a form of communication and it is a skill at which everyone can become competent. Board writing needs to be big enough for all to see, legible, and straight, so it helps for you to go to the back of the room to check from time to time.

If you do not have equipment such as an OVERHEAD PROJECTOR (OHP) or a computer with a data projector available and you need a lot of writing on the board for your next lesson, consider checking if the room is free beforehand and doing the writing in advance. It is true that this takes time, but it creates a relaxed starting point to the lesson and also makes for a good atmosphere if students find the teacher there working for them as they arrive.

It is also important to plan how to use the board. The pressure of using it in front of students can lead to disorganized scribbles, or to rubbing out something that is needed later. One basic strategy is to use different parts of the board for different things. The right-hand half of the board can be reserved for the work you have planned, a left-hand column for new words which come up during the lesson, and the space in between for impromptu

Figure 5.4 An example of organized board work

examples, diagrams, and so on. This establishes a recognizable order to help you and your class communicate via the board. Figure 5.4 shows an example of a board organized in this way.

The teacher should not be possessive about the board. Students can often make very good use of it, too. There are many ways students can participate in board use. For example, in a reading class with a text about marriage, the lesson could start with the teacher saying *I'm going to write a word on the board. Then you come out and write down the first word you think of when I write my word.* (The teacher writes the word 'marriage' on the board.) What would probably result from this?

- *Movement round the classroom.* This technique might be useful in a situation where the students have been sitting for a while.
- *Involvement.* The students are contributing to the lesson, although they may not yet know how.
- *Engagement.* The students are sharing a personal reaction which will also start them thinking about the topic. This preparatory thinking will ease their way into understanding the passage.
- *Skills.* One way to start work on the passage would be to have students SCAN it in order to look for the blackboard words in the passage.

On another occasion, a student might ask *How do you pronounce this word?* A useful thing for the student to do is to write it on the board, over on the left where the new words go. Or the teacher might have collected a few ERRORS students have made in their writing and a student can be asked to write them on the board while the teacher does something else. Or if an activity involves some kind of competition, one or two students can be at the board keeping score. If, during break time, students think of something they wish they could say in English, they can write it on the board in order to remind themselves to ask the teacher.

In short, make the board available to students. It is worth keeping this simple but powerful principle in mind as we look at other items of ELT equipment. And, of course, in the interests of good relations among colleagues, it is always a good idea to clean the board before you leave!

Technology

Contemporary ELT has a lot of electrical and electronic equipment available for use; until relatively recently the most common items were the overhead projector, the audiocassette player, and the videocassette player. Now there are also CD players, DVD players, interactive whiteboards, MP3 players, and computer facilities such as PowerPoint and the Internet, as well as computer laboratories. The list could go on. Some teachers will be faced with all these machines from the very beginning of their careers. Some may never see any of them in their classrooms. We shall make some general points about them all, followed by a few detailed comments on each.

Unlike the board, all these modern pieces of equipment can go wrong, as can the electricity supply itself. So before the class, the teacher needs to make sure that the equipment is in the right place and that it is working. It is also necessary to check that the material is ready and works on that particular machine.

If the machine then breaks down, the students will probably be sympathetic, but they will still need teaching. So it is a good idea to be familiar with the basics of how the machine works, and to know who to contact for help. It may well be that one of the students can fix it – they often know more about the technology than the teacher does!

If the machine still does not work, the question is what can you do right now? There are three options:

1 use the same material some other way (for example, read out a dialogue)
2 move on to another part of the coursebook or teaching programme
3 have a 'safety-net' lesson ready for use at any time. (Storytelling can be useful here. For example, have a story of your own 'equipment worst nightmare' ready, after which students might want to share their own technology misadventures and breakdowns.)

Technology offers many opportunities to enhance learning, so it would be a pity not to exploit at least some of its potential. If you are somewhat reluctant to take the plunge, try not to let unfamiliar equipment put you off. A DVD player is no more complicated or difficult to operate than a videocassette player.

Here are some general points about first approaches:

- Ask a colleague to show you how something works. Other teachers are often afraid of 'interfering', but are also often happy to help if asked, especially with something they are enthusiastic about.
- Spend some time familiarizing yourself with the equipment. Do not underestimate the importance of hands-on experience.
- Experience the equipment from the learner's point of view. Sit in the computer laboratory, for example, and go through the materials and experience them as a student does.
- Look out for opportunities to let students work the equipment in class. Getting them to carry out simple mechanical tasks can be quite extraordinary in turning them into participants.
- Ask if your school can organize training or seminars on using new technologies in ELT.

It is worth remembering that the equipment we are considering here shares one common feature with all language teaching materials. The first question is *How do I use this?* but the next and more important question is *Why do I use this?* If you do not ask yourself this, your students may find themselves sitting in front of computer screens just because the school has the technology. In this scenario, what should be an aid to learning simply becomes a high-tech way of passing the time. The key is to keep on asking how the use of equipment relates to the underlying motivational aspects of *communication, feelings, rules, practice,* and *strategies.*

In the brief notes that follow, therefore, we shall concentrate on *why* one would want to use these machines. We shall leave you to follow up the details of *how* to use them if it is useful to do so in your setting.

The overhead projector/computer presentations

Both the overhead projector (OHP) and computer presentation facilities such as PowerPoint have two very positive characteristics:

1 written material or visual aids can be prepared before the class
2 the teacher can face the students while writing or pointing things out.

The interactive whiteboard also has these characteristics, but we will deal with that piece of equipment separately below.

Again, it is important not to be possessive about this equipment. The overhead transparency (OHT) is a useful way of having a group present notes on work they have done in class. Or if one group member has been listening out for mistakes during an activity, these can be written on an OHT for the whole class to discuss. A computer with PowerPoint and a data projector can be used for group presentations as well as for noting key points during class discussions. Students can be asked to prepare PowerPoint slides in groups in the computer lab or for homework to present in a subsequent lesson.

In each situation, the teacher needs to remind students to check their print size to ensure that everyone in the class will be able to see clearly.

Audio equipment

As we noted above, the range of audio equipment found in a classroom today can be extremely wide. Our approach will be to discuss audio equipment in general, as it is the 'audio' element itself that matters in language learning, not so much the type of equipment that delivers it.

All audio equipment is useful in that it can provide a class with a range of voices and interactions. Recordings can consist of male and female voices, with a variety of regional accents. They might be in the form of monologues, dialogues, or multi-party talk in different registers. The variety itself is important and helps learners to develop their sense of appropriacy and flexibility.

Such recordings are often central to the presentation of new language (see Chapter 8), and to the provision of listening practice (see Chapter 9). When you bring in outside materials, encourage your students to do the same. You may have to listen to some songs you might otherwise not have chosen to listen to, but if your students are thinking about recording English, they are likely to be listening to whatever English is available to them.

As well as bringing the outside world into the classroom, digital recorders can be used to help students concentrate on the English they use in the classroom. Groups can be recorded during an activity. This may cause awkwardness at first, but students soon get used to it. The recording can be used in a variety of ways, for example:

- The group members take the recording home and listen to themselves on their MP3 players or mobile phones. Each one then later tells the teacher one thing they have learnt from listening to the recording.
- While the rest of the class carries out the next activity, one group works together on the recording. They prepare to report back to the class on things they thought the others said really well, or point out mistakes they noticed and corrected, and on.

Where a good digital recorder is available, this can also be used to make POD-CASTS. These are digital recordings on a particular topic, which are then posted on the Internet. Generally, they are publicly available, but this raises all sorts of safety and ethical issues. One possibility is to use one of the many sites where students can have a class BLOG, which is password-protected. Here they can post their podcasts and other work available to be viewed only by those who have the password. Another alternative is to have a class or school WIKI for the same purpose. All these features can be very motivating for learners, but the teacher needs to keep a careful eye on what is being posted and where.

MP3 players are a part of everyday life for a great many people. People can and do listen to them while walking, driving, and lying in bed. You simply need to apply your ingenuity to motivate your students to listen to English. Apart from enabling students to take classroom recordings home, MP3 players also encourage students to work out the words to their favourite songs or to download the words from the Internet. At this point, students can listen, read, or sing along at the same time. If they encounter any language difficulties, they can then bring them to class to discuss with the group.

Video equipment

The points we made about audio equipment are equally valid for video equipment. The old VHS has been overtaken by DVDs, but the principles underlying their use in the classroom are the same.

Video provides visual and aural information at the same time, so students are able to see communication in action. It also gives teachers a chance to separate vision and sound in the teaching of language in use; a particular video clip can be chosen to focus initially on particular language functions. At its simplest, a brief exchange can be shown on screen without sound and the teacher asks the students first *What are they doing?* and then *What are they saying?*

In the discussion of what the characters are doing, the teacher can draw attention to typical facial expressions, gestures, or body movements. When predicting what people are saying, the students' attention can also be drawn to the social appropriacy of different ways of expressing the functions. For example, if the students think that one person has asked another to do something, they can be asked what the most suitable form of request would be. When the teacher then plays the sequence with sound, the students have a very good reason to listen carefully. For variety, this procedure can be reversed, with only the sound played first. The students then have to predict the situation, characters, action, and relationships involved.

People spend a lot of time watching television and are probably used to reasonably high quality sound and vision. Poor quality in these areas can be very demotivating. Moreover, people have their own television-watching habits, which are probably very different from concentrated viewing-for-learning. Teaching with video has to be distinguished from watching television. So it is a good idea to keep video extracts short, and ensure that students have something to look out for to give them a good reason for viewing.

In addition to commercial video material and television programmes that can be recorded (with the necessary permissions), the Internet is a good source of short instructional video clips. We mentioned *Videojug* in Chapter 4 and, in spite of its growing notoriety, *YouTube* also contains useful clips.

If a video camera is available, students could make and edit their own films to post on the school intranet or simply to share with the rest of the class or school. Even if there is no video camera, most digital cameras can be used to record video, as can most mobile phones. The capability is limited and the quality, especially of mobile phones, may not be as high as a video camera, but they can be useful for recording short snippets, and the sense of ownership and involvement can be intrinsically motivating.

The interactive whiteboard

Potentially, the interactive whiteboard could be the only piece of equipment you need. It can do the same job as a traditional board, a FLIPCHART, an OHP, a computer presentation, any piece of audio and video equipment, and much more. Moreover, it is *interactive*, as its name suggests. Learners can write on it, or the teacher can add ideas; any changes can be saved and returned to later. Screens can also be printed so that learners have a record of their work. There are specific software packages, some downloadable free from the Internet, that can be used with the interactive whiteboard. Finally, publishers are increasingly producing digital versions of their coursebooks for use with the interactive whiteboard. For example, pages from the coursebook can be projected for the whole class to see and for the teacher (or students) to write on, while audio files can be played at the same time.

Learners generally find the interactive whiteboard very engaging and motivating. Teachers may find it time-consuming initially, as they have to get used to using it and preparing new lessons; but ultimately it probably saves time because a bank of lessons and materials can be built up to use relatively quickly and easily.

As with all technology, however, you need to ask yourself how it fits in with the aims of the lesson. The best use of the interactive whiteboard (and indeed of any other equipment) is one where it is fully integrated with the learning objectives and not used just because it is there.

Computer laboratories

If a computer laboratory where learners can work on the computers is available, there are many ways of enhancing their language-learning experience, including giving them projects to do on the Internet. For example, teachers can:

- Give the students a list of items to 'buy' on the Internet and see who can complete the list at the lowest price in the shortest time (making sure they do not actually buy anything, of course!)

- Give them a list of questions to answer on a particular subject area, such as geography, history, or current affairs.
- Ask them to plan a holiday for a specific group of people, drawing up the itinerary, finding hotels, restaurants, and places of interest to visit.
- Set up online projects with partner schools in other countries.

As well as interacting individually with the computer, students can also work in pairs, two to a computer, so that they interact with each other to complete the task(s).

The computer laboratory can also be used to 'chat'. Students who are reluctant to speak in class are often happy to 'chat' on the computer, exchanging messages with their classmates. Of course, chatting on a computer is not the same as chatting face to face, but it can be a way of encouraging self-confidence. Teachers can also find key-pals (an electronic version of pen-pals), for their students to chat with or write in English to students from other countries. There are websites dedicated to this.

Virtual learning environments (VLEs)

VLEs are software systems that are used to organize, manage, and support learning. They typically have areas for content, discussion forums, exercises, and assessment, among other things.

The teacher can use the VLE to post extra exercises for the students to do for homework, or as extra practice for those who need it. In this way, the VLE can help the teacher to individualize learning. VLEs can also be used to create fairly simple exercises such as MULTIPLE-CHOICE QUESTIONS or GAP FILLS, for example. Students can monitor their own progress with the automatic exercise correction and assessment facility.

The VLE also lends itself to project work. Students can be put into groups and assigned a particular project. The teacher creates a discussion forum for each group where the members can cooperate virtually with each other. In order for these discussion forums to work well, students need to be given an incentive to post their contributions. This can be done either by assessing their postings, or by setting a minimum number of contributions each student has to make every week. An even better alternative is to give a different student responsibility for the forum, topic, or discussion thread each week. That student then has to ensure that the discussion takes place and that the task is completed.

All this means that organized learning is not necessarily confined to a limited number of hours each week in the classroom. In essence, you become a 24/7 teacher!

Then of course there are all the possibilities available to learners on their mobile phones and computers at home: text messaging, blogs, wikis, web pages, and so on. More and more is becoming available all the time. By the time you read this chapter, some of what we have said may already be out of date; it will be up to you to find new options.

Summary

In this chapter we have looked at different aspects of the learning and teaching environment. We started by looking at the physical space; we then touched on all the equipment that might be available to the teacher; and finally we discussed a few of the things that can be done with that equipment to enhance students' learning experience.

The overall message is that the learning environment can and will exert a powerful influence on the teaching and learning that take place. It is therefore important to make yourself thoroughly at ease with your teaching space and with the equipment you intend to use.

Think carefully about the equipment you have and how it might be useful to your teaching and to your students' learning. The equipment has to be an aid to attaining the learning objectives; the objectives should not be designed to fit the equipment. Do not feel that you have to use it just because it is there. Equally, do not feel that just because you do not have the latest equipment available, your teaching or your learners' learning experience is somehow inferior. It is not. The teacher's creativity is the key in both cases.

We have now completed our familiarization with the ELT classroom, and have also noted some principles and procedures that are useful when we want to ensure that the elements of that classroom interact. That was the easy part.

Questions and activities

Think about your responses and then discuss them with a colleague if possible.

1 Think about classrooms in which you have studied. Do you agree that the room and its furniture had an effect either on the work that was done there or your enjoyment of it? Can you give examples?

2 Much of what is said about furniture and interaction has an ideological base: it assumes that giving people freedom and responsibility is a good thing. Is this necessarily the case everywhere? In an authoritarian society, could this cause problems? What problems might it cause? What do you learn from this?

3 What problems might you come up against if you follow the suggestion to 'make the board available'? How would do you react to these?

4 What experience do you have as a learner or as a teacher of the equipment written about in this chapter? How do you feel about using it? Note
   down any problems, questions, or ideas you have and discuss them with
   a colleague.
5 If some of the equipment described in this chapter is not available to you,
   did you notice anything which suggests that some things cannot be done
   without that equipment? If so, write them down and think about ways of
   achieving the same learning opportunities without the technology.

There is no key for this chapter because all the questions above are reflective/
practical and depend either on experience or the materials found by each
teacher.

PART TWO

Action

In Part One of this book, we observed the main elements of any ELT situation and looked at examples of teaching techniques. In Part Two, we concentrate more directly on methodology and teaching procedures and take the presence of the main elements as given.

We now look at how to:

- plan and manage classroom activity
- organize learning through communication
- introduce and practise new language
- choose appropriate techniques for correction
- teach the skills of listening, speaking, reading, and writing
- use tests and teach in the context of formal examinations
- continue personal and professional development in ELT.

Before we explore any of those topics, however, we need to make some introductory comments to paint in the broad background against which this action will take place.

Managing teaching and learning

In Chapter 2 we suggested that choosing what to teach, listing aims and objectives, and preparing appropriate activities to fulfil those aims and objectives will not always deliver specific outcomes in terms of learning. Nevertheless, these steps can still be useful in terms of organizing teaching, and organized teaching can help create a secure environment for learning. Learners may not learn what teachers think they have taught them at a conscious level, but they may well have learnt something else at a subconscious level.

Whatever type of teaching/learning activity your class is engaged in, your students will be dependent on your skills as a *manager* of what is going on. It is for this reason that we begin the second part of this book with a chapter on classroom management.

Communication and language

Also in Chapter 2, we suggested that there are two broad methodological approaches to language teaching. In Chapter 7, we show how in the first of these approaches, the teacher moves from *communication* to *language*, giving the students a task, encouraging them to communicate, and focusing on specific forms where necessary. In the second approach, discussed in Chapter 8, the teacher moves from *language* to *communication*, introducing parts of the language, practising them, and personalizing them.

We do *not* mean to suggest that teachers should choose one or other of these directions and stick to it. Any sensible approach to language teaching will use elements of both. As a very general guide, the following observations can be made. See how they match up with your experience:

- The more language learners already know, the more often it makes sense to engage them directly in communicative activities to see where they need formal support.
- The less language learners already know, the more often it makes sense to introduce new language forms for them to learn to use.
- It can also be effective to use a task-first approach with elementary learners, and to present a specific item of language form to advanced learners.
- If the learners are used to being taught in one of the above ways, it makes sense to go along with the style they know and then gradually introduce the alternative.
- If the learners have reached a new stage in their education (for example, they have just left school and started college or university, or started vocational training), that might be the perfect time to introduce a task-based approach, as it fits in with their likely desire to experience change and new, more adult directions.

As you can see, there are no hard and fast rules in this area, because there is no one-size-fits-all method of language teaching. Wherever you enter the cycle of language and communication, the two approaches should support each other in a continuing fashion.

In Chapters 7 and 8 we will be looking in more detail at the two broad approaches to language teaching that we introduced in Chapter 2.

A developmental attitude

Finally, this book can offer *ways* of doing things, but not *the* way of doing them. Every idea can be improved on and adapted. And once you have found out which procedures suit you and your students best, it is a good idea to use others at times. Variety of method is both a part of good teaching and a basis for the teacher's own development. The issue of teacher development is the theme of our final chapter. This book aims to follow the methodological principle underlying all the teaching suggestions in it: we begin with the learner and what the learner knows, move with the learner into the unknown, and then focus again on the learner to ask *What can you do now?* The same exploratory principle applies to our own and your professional development.

The overall purpose of this book is to help more teacher-learners decide for themselves what their next steps will be. In the following chapters, you will see the importance of the issues we have discussed. Your part is to continue to relate the generalities of the book to the specifics of your own experience. Having done that, you need to ask yourself how you would now express the knowledge you have developed. The subsequent step is to base your future action on that new understanding.

6 CLASSROOM MANAGEMENT

In Chapter 5, we talked about how and why teachers might use the equipment available to them. In this chapter, we look at ways of managing the events and the people. We shall focus on the *planning, interactions*, and *language* of classroom management. In practice, these issues are not separate from methodology. We have separated them in order to focus on them clearly now, and to concentrate on other aspects of teaching methods in the chapters which follow.

Planning

In this section, we concentrate on lesson plans, but first we need to examine two aspects of a broader picture.

First, even teachers who have no planning responsibilities beyond their own classes still need to have a scheme of work. Their planning needs to extend beyond the end of the next lesson to include a sequence of lessons.

Teachers need an overview of the goals they and their students aim to achieve over a series of lessons, or a whole course. If they are working with published or previously prepared materials, this might only be in terms of the units they are going to cover. But it is always a good idea to SKIM through a coursebook, or read through the materials and the teacher's guide in some detail at least to the end of the next unit in order to have an overview of what is coming up. This is not idealistic advice – it is good survival strategy. You can feel very silly if you cannot answer a question today which the book raises tomorrow.

In some teaching situations, forward planning is more difficult. If teachers find themselves teaching a sequence of unconnected lessons where they have to deal with whatever turns up, it is a good idea to pause after every few lessons and, together with the students, review and record what has been covered. The headings *lexis, grammar, functions, pronunciation*, and *discourse* might be used, together with any useful *strategies*. In this way, the teacher will give shape to what has been done and connections will begin to emerge. This will certainly also help students to remember and consolidate new language.

Second, it is always worth finding out about students' needs and preferences, their backgrounds and motivations, and then drawing up LEARNER PROFILES and a CLASS PROFILE to help with planning. Figure 6.1 is an example of a questionnaire used with groups of international students studying English at a British university. Needs assessment can inform the teacher and raise learners' awareness of the situations in which they use English, the skills they need, and what is most important for them to work on. This should help with planning a course, choosing supplementary materials to add to what a coursebook offers, and help students to focus their learning efforts.

Questionnaire

Please answer the following questions. Your responses will be used in planning the English language programme. Thank you for your cooperation.

1   How long have you been living in the UK?

2   What course/modules are you taking this year?

3   Do you have an IELTS or a TOEFL score? Yes ☐ No ☐

   If yes, please write your score below:

   TOEFL:
   IELTS Bandscore: Listening: Speaking: Reading: Writing:

4   What language areas do you need help with in particular?
   Please tick (✓) as appropriate.

Improving my	no help	a little help	some help	a lot of help
Reading skills				
Listening skills				
Speaking skills				
Writing skills				
Grammar				
Vocabulary				
Pronunciation				
Punctuation				
Answering exam questions				
Oral presentation skills				
Telephone skills				
Use of everyday language				

Figure 6.1 A needs-assessment questionnaire

It is worth remembering that students' perception of their needs can change over time, so a needs assessment should be carried out at regular intervals. This enables the teacher to adjust his or her teaching according to what the students think they need, as well as what the teacher thinks they need.

A questionnaire such as the one in Figure 6.1, suitably adjusted for context, can also be used to help students draw up individual learning plans, which they can then refer to in order to monitor their progress throughout the course. This can be reviewed and revised at regular intervals as each student's needs change.

Lesson plans

We shall concentrate on the lesson plan as a practical working document. If you are studying for a teaching certificate of some kind, you will probably find that your ability to produce a lesson plan is part of your assessment. In these circumstances, you need to find out exactly what your lesson plans should contain, how they should be laid out, and how they will be assessed. The points made here will underlie any more complicated model which you are asked to produce for examination purposes.

The process of writing a lesson plan should help you clarify your answers to the following questions:

1 What are the aims of this lesson?
2 How am I going to achieve these aims?
3 How will I know if I have achieved my aims or not?

The lesson plan itself should then act as a reminder during the lesson of your answers to these questions. We will first look at the questions in more detail and then put a plan together.

What are the aims of this lesson?

There are two ways of looking at this. Aims can be stated in terms of what the teacher intends to cover in a lesson. More demandingly, objectives can be stated in terms of what the teacher wants the students to be able to do by the end of the lesson.

So, for example, a possible *aim* might be:

To introduce the names of items of clothing

While a possible *objective* might be:

By the end of this lesson, students will be able to name all the items of clothing worn by students in this class.

Despite what we have said about students not necessarily learning what teachers want to teach them, this kind of statement of objectives does give both students and teachers something that they can check. They then all have a clear idea of what progress is or is not being made in terms of what the students *can do*. This is probably more interesting in the long run than what teachers have aimed to do. This use of *objectives* also provides a way of answering the third question above: *How will I know if I have achieved my aims or not?*

Sometimes a lesson may also have subsidiary aims. So, for example, if the main aim of the lesson is:

To introduce the different uses of 'like' in questions

Subsidiary aims may be:

To practise sentence stress and intonation in questions

To revise descriptions of people, food, and places

It is important to keep thinking about what the students will be able to do, even though it is not always possible to predict accurately. If the aim of a lesson is vague, such as 'to give further practice of reading skills', then so be it. However, perhaps you can better focus your thinking (and your teaching) if you try to be more specific in your objectives. For example:

By the end of this lesson, students will have had further practice in:

- skimming to get an overall sense of a text
- improving their reading speed by timed reading
- justifying answers to questions by reference to the text
- relating the content of the text to their own experience.

It may also be useful for the teacher to identify some personal aims for the lesson, to further professional development and improve teaching. An example of a personal aim might be something like:

To experiment with different ways of checking that learners have understood my instructions

When planning a lesson, it is also a good idea to think about what assumptions can be made about what the learners know and do not know, and what language problems they may have with the lesson. For example, returning to the aim:

To introduce the different uses of 'like' in questions

The teacher might assume that students are already familiar with question forms. They will also be familiar with the question 'What does he/she like?' and the present simple tense.

The teacher might anticipate that students will mix up the form of the questions and will have problems distinguishing the meaning of the various questions with like: *What is he/she like? What does he/she like? What does he/she look like?*

By thinking carefully beforehand and anticipating language problems, the teacher is better prepared to deal with them if and when they arise.

So the first part of a lesson plan might look something like this:

Lesson plan
Class: Intermediate   **Date:** 29 October   **Time:** 11.00–12.30

Lesson aims
To introduce the different uses of *like* in questions; to revise descriptions of people, food, and places.

Lesson objectives
By the end of the lesson students will:
- be able to ask about and describe people's appearance, personality, and state of well-being
- show awareness of the differences in form and meaning of questions with *like*.

Personal aims
To experiment with different students groupings, so they work with different people.

Topic/function	**New vocabulary**	**Anticipated problems**
Talking about people	No new vocabulary; revision of vocabulary to do with appearances and personality	• Students may have difficulty with the form of the questions.
New structures *What is ... like?* *What does ... look like?*		• Students may confuse the meaning of the various questions with like.
Phonology points Sentence stress and intonation in questions		• Students may make mistakes in word order (adjective + noun).
		• Students may not be familiar with the order of adjectives (*brown short hair).

Figure 6.2 Part of a lesson plan

How am I going to achieve these aims and objectives?

This is the main body of the plan, where the various steps of the lesson relate to

- what the teacher is going to do
- what the students are going to do
- how long each step is going to take.

Whatever the specific focus of the lesson is, each lesson should feature good RAPPORT. This will not appear on the lesson plan itself, but that does not make it less important. What the appropriate relationships are will depend on you, your students, and the context in which you work; but always allow time for the greetings and personal exchanges that acknowledge each lesson as a social event.

Sometimes these exchanges will be enough to get the students settled and ready to start work. At other times, it helps to use a short introductory activity to warm up the students, bring the class together, and prepare them to start the lesson. These warmers can be quick and fun. Once you try some out, you will develop ideas that suit your own way of being a teacher. Here are three examples:

1 Physical
Students come to the front of the class and line up in birthday order. (However, this does involve a lot of movement with minimal communication. Large classes can be divided into two or more groups at the front and back of the classroom.)
2 Intellectual
Simple mathematical problems can be used here, for example:

- *What's four times two? Plus eight? Times three? Divided by twelve? Plus thirty-seven? Minus eighteen?*

3 Personal
A good icebreaker when a new class meets for the first time invites students to MINGLE and get to know each other. In 'Find someone who …' the teacher prepares a number of statements and asks the students to find someone who, for example:

- can play a musical instrument
- likes getting up early in the morning
- can speak more than two languages.

The students walk around the room asking each other the relevant questions until they find a different person who fits each of the statements. This works especially well if the teacher can find out something specific about each student beforehand and use that information to prepare the statements.

Alternatively, an introductory activity might be revision of the previous lesson, or be more closely linked to the aims of the new lesson and act as a lead-in to it. This is the case of the introductory question in the lesson plan below. Whatever activity you do, as the lesson gets under way, it is often a good idea to refer back to a related previous lesson. Recycling earlier material helps students to remember and learn it. It also helps them make connections between what they know already and what they are about to learn. If nothing else, it gets the students back into 'English lesson' mode. Then the teacher can get on with the main purpose of the current lesson.

One clear layout for a lesson plan is to set it up in five columns: one for the teacher, one to show the interaction patterns between the teacher and students, one for the students, one for the aims of the activity, and one for timing. Whether interactions are written separately or not, it is important that any plan should anticipate and provide for a variety of interaction as the lesson proceeds. We shall be discussing interaction in greater detail later in the chapter.

How will I know if I have achieved my aims and objectives or not?

The more specifically the objectives of the lesson have been set out in terms of what the students will be able to do, the easier it is to check them. If the aim of the lesson is *to introduce the different uses of 'like' in questions*, then a possible way of checking at the end of the lesson is outlined in Figure 6.3. These are two short and simple activities, both of which are designed to check what the students have learnt. As we said earlier, students will not necessarily have learnt exactly what the teacher thinks he or she has taught them, but a short checking activity at the end of the lesson will show just what they have learnt in this area.

These timings can only be approximate, but in general it is important to get timings as accurate as possible. A great teacher fear is of not having enough

Teacher's activity	T↔S? S↔S?	Students' activity	Aim	Timing
Put students in pairs. Give out cards with answers to the three questions with *like*.	T→S		To check if students have learnt the differences in the question forms during the lesson.	2 minutes
	S→S	Students take it in turns to pick up a card and ask the correct question.		5 minutes
Nominate a student and ask one of these questions: *Who do you look like? Who does your sister/ brother/mother look like? What is your best friend like?* etc.	T→S	Nominated student answers the question.		2 minutes

Figure 6.3 An aims achievement checklist

material, leading to lessons over-full of material. The result may be an incomplete lesson where the learners do not actually get as far as using the main teaching point of the lesson for themselves. Or the teacher rushes through the activities without exploiting the full potential of the materials and without giving the learners the time they really need to spend on each activity.

In a normal teaching situation, what does not get done this lesson can often be pushed into the next lesson without any great problem. But if this happens on a regular basis, as the weeks go by, it becomes clear that students are not going to reach the stage they were supposed to reach by the end of the term or the course.

The key is to plan the timings for each stage as carefully as possible, and take the trouble to write in the real timings afterwards. Another option is to have some extra activities that are not an integral part of the lesson, but that can be drawn on if there is time left over at the end of a lesson. In continuing to

6 I just love it!

like · Verb patterns · Describing food, towns, and people · Signs and sounds

▶ **TEST YOUR GRAMMAR**

1 Complete these sentences about you.

1 I look just like my . . .	4 After this class, I'd like to . . .
2 I like my coffee . . .	5 When I'm on holiday, I enjoy . . .
3 On Sundays, I like . . .	6 Yesterday evening, I decided to . . .

2 Tell the class some of the things you wrote.

> *I look just like my father.*

A STUDENT VISITOR
Questions with *like*

1 Many students go to study in a foreign country. Do you know anyone who has studied abroad?

2 Sandy and her friend Nina in Melbourne, Australia, are talking about a student visitor from South Korea. Complete the conversation using these questions.

What does she like doing?	How is she now?	What's she like?
What does she look like?	What would she like to do?	

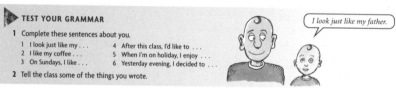

Sandy Our student from Seoul arrived on Monday.
Nina What's her name?
Sandy Soon-hee.
Nina That's a pretty name! (1)_____
Sandy She's really nice. I'm sure we'll get on well. We seem to have a lot in common.
Nina How do you know that already? (2)_____
Sandy Well, she likes photography, and so do I. And we both like listening to the same kind of music.
Nina (3)_____
Sandy Oh, she's really pretty. She has big, brown eyes and long, dark hair.

Nina Why don't we do something with Soon-hee this weekend? What should we do? Get a pizza? Go shopping? (4)_____
Sandy I'll ask her tonight. She was a bit homesick at first, so I'm pretty sure she'll want to go out and make some friends.
Nina (5)_____
Sandy Oh, she's OK. She called her parents and she felt much better after she'd spoken to them.
Nina Oh, that's good. I can't wait to meet her.

T 6.1 Listen and check. Practise the conversation with a partner.

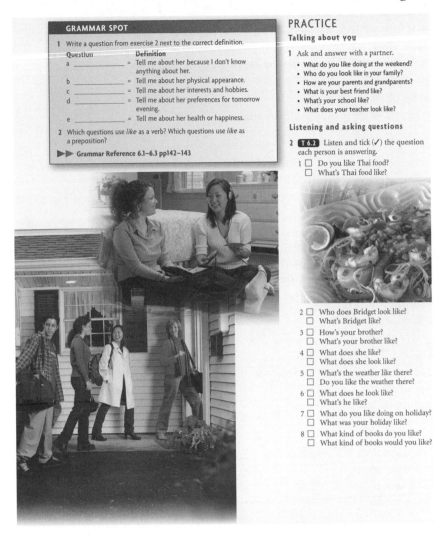

GRAMMAR SPOT

1 Write a question from exercise 2 next to the correct definition.

Question	Definition
a _____	= Tell me about her because I don't know anything about her.
b _____	= Tell me about her physical appearance.
c _____	= Tell me about her interests and hobbies.
d _____	= Tell me about her preferences for tomorrow evening.
e _____	= Tell me about her health or happiness.

2 Which questions use *like* as a verb? Which questions use *like* as a preposition?

▶▶ Grammar Reference 6.1–6.3 pp142–143

PRACTICE

Talking about you

1 Ask and answer with a partner.
 • What do you like doing at the weekend?
 • Who do you look like in your family?
 • How are your parents and grandparents?
 • What is your best friend like?
 • What's your school like?
 • What does your teacher look like?

Listening and asking questions

2 **T 6.2** Listen and tick (✓) the question each person is answering.
 1 ☐ Do you like Thai food?
   ☐ What's Thai food like?
 2 ☐ Who does Bridget look like?
   ☐ What's Bridget like?
 3 ☐ How's your brother?
   ☐ What's your brother like?
 4 ☐ What does she like?
   ☐ What does she look like?
 5 ☐ What's the weather like there?
   ☐ Do you like the weather there?
 6 ☐ What does he look like?
   ☐ What's he like?
 7 ☐ What do you like doing on holiday?
   ☐ What was your holiday like?
 8 ☐ What kind of books do you like?
   ☐ What kind of books would you like?

Materials extract 6.1 Soars and Soars: Headway Intermediate, pages 46–47

develop an informed sense of what is likely to be achieved in real time, you are developing a skill that will be invaluable if you become involved in course planning. Let us now look at some materials in Materials extract 6.1 written for adults who are at intermediate level and who have progressed to Unit 6 of their coursebook and see what a possible lesson plan might look like.

The lesson plan in Figure 6.4 below is complete with all its components, and is the continuation of the first part of the lesson plan shown in Figure 6.2. The aims and objectives have been repeated here for ease of reference. We start off the lesson and then invite you to turn to the questions and activities at the end of the chapter (Question 5).

Lesson plan

Class: Intermediate   **Date:** 29 October   **Time:** 11.00–12.30

Lesson aims

To introduce the different uses of *like* in questions; to revise descriptions of people, food, and places

Lesson objectives

By the end of the lesson students will:
• be able to ask about and describe people's appearance, personality, and state of well-being
• show awareness of the differences in form and meaning of questions with *like*.

Personal aims

To experiment with different students groupings, so they work with different people

Topic/function	New vocabulary	Anticipated problems
Talking about people	No new vocabulary	• Students may have difficulty with the form of the questions.
New structures	Revision of vocabulary to do with appearances and personality	• Students may confuse the meaning of the various questions with *like*.
What is ... like?		• Students may make mistakes in word order (adjective + noun).
What does ... look like?		
Phonology points		• Students may not be familiar with the order of adjectives (*brown short hair).
Sentence stress and intonation in questions		

Teacher's activity	T↔S? S↔S?	Students' activity	Aim	Timing
1 Nominate two or three students and ask them who they look like.	T→S	Nominated students respond.	To see how much students already know.	11.00
Ask students to complete sentences. Elicit answers for each sentence.	T→S	Students complete the sentences individually.		11.15
2 Ask question 1. Elicit answers about what the student liked, etc.	T→Ss	Respond.	Lead-in to main language point of the lesson.	
			Introduce the different questions inductively.	11.22
3 Ask students to complete the conversation in Exercise 2 in pairs.	T→Ss S↔S	Fill in the gaps.		
4 Play the recording so that students can check their answers.	T→Ss	Check answers.		

Figure 6.4 Complete lesson plan

It is highly unlikely that an experienced teacher would write out anything as explicit as this plan, for two good reasons. First, this plan was written to communicate with someone else, while a practical lesson plan is written only for the use of its writer. Second, the more experienced the teacher, the easier it is to write a short note that will be meaningful to that teacher. But this is *not* an argument against writing lesson plans. Students depend on teachers to have a clear sense of purpose and a means of proceeding towards that purpose in real time. Both as a way of preparing yourself to teach, and helping you teach, we know of no substitute for a lesson plan, and it pays to begin with a clear and explicit framework.

On our plan, we have marked the intended teacher ↔ student and student ↔ student interactions. This is a key aspect of classroom management. Let us now look at this in more detail.

Interactions

When we talk about different INTERACTION PATTERNS in class, we mean who is speaking to whom. Here are some common examples:

The teacher sometimes gives instructions to the whole class (T→Ss) and sometimes to an individual (T→S). Sometimes, there will be an exchange between the teacher and the whole class (T↔Ss) and sometimes the teacher will tell one student to say something to another (T→S→S). Sometimes, students will communicate directly with each other (S↔S). Ideally there will also be communication with the teacher initiated by the students (S↔T), but this is a pattern that can only be encouraged not planned. A movement from interaction between the teacher and the whole class to interaction between students themselves (either in pairs or groups) is the most usual pattern of interaction in ELT. Using language in different *interactions* is as important to language learning as studying different *forms* of language.

Other advantages of varying the interactions in classroom teaching are:

- changes of interaction bring a change of pace and focus, and that helps to keep students interested and their energy levels high
- pair and groupwork provides opportunities for many more individuals to use the language, and also decreases TEACHER TALKING TIME (TTT)
- students perform differently without the pressure of teacher and whole-class attention
- students learn to be more self-reliant
- teachers get a chance to listen and evaluate what has been learnt if the focus of attention is off them.

Teacher to student(s)

In teacher-fronted interaction, the teacher leads the class in an activity, and this is where there is most control over the lesson and over what learners say.

At this point, you might like to look back at the examples we gave for each of the teacher roles we identified in Chapter 1. With one exception, the examples are all taken from such open class situations.

What about the language teachers use? First, experienced teachers grade their language to suit the level of the learners they are teaching. This can be one of the most difficult aspects of teacher talk when you first start teaching. Looking back at the examples in Chapter 1 again, two of them are from a lower-level class than the others. Can you tell which?

Second, a very common classroom interaction pattern is one where the teacher asks a question, the student or students respond and the teacher gives some sort of indication as to whether the answer was acceptable or not. This is called the Initiation Response Feedback (IRF) pattern (Sinclair and Coulthard 1975) and is common in all classrooms, not only language classrooms. Here is an example:

TEACHER   Could we think of another word with a similar meaning to 'abundant'?
ARI   'Plenty of'
TEACHER   'Plenty of' would be a good one. Which one is a positive word?
STUDENTS   'Abundant'
TEACHER   Abundant, yes. And 'redundant' is?
STUDENTS   Negative
TEACHER   Negative. Yeah. Generally speaking, it's a negative word. Try and think of it like that.

This form of interaction is completely teacher-centred. The teacher is very much in control and the learners have a passive rather than an active role, as they are only responding to something the teacher initiates. Moreover, there are few opportunities for most of the students to say anything because often only one student can speak at a time. On the other hand, as a way of organizing and checking learning, making sure that everyone is on-task and moving the lesson forward, such interaction is undoubtedly useful. In these terms, the above exchanges can be seen as positive communicative interactions in classroom-based English. As with so many other aspects of language teaching, it is a question of balance.

Student(s) to student(s)

Some teachers worry about their lack of control when they use pair-work or groupwork, because they no longer have the students' undivided attention and therefore cannot have direct control over each individual. This, we suggest, is to misunderstand the teacher's role and power. The teacher is not asked to give up control in order to use pairwork and groupwork. The teacher is asked to exercise a different kind of control (self-control and organization) in order to use pairwork and groupwork. This is the kind of relationship that we talked about in Chapter 2, where the teacher's control is used to increase the learner's freedom and opportunity to learn (see page 25).

However, introducing pairwork or groupwork in a situation where it has not been used before can be difficult for two main reasons:

1 conflict with the students' ideas of what 'being taught' means
2 conflict with colleagues' ideas of what 'being a teacher' means.

These are not arguments against introducing pairwork and groupwork, but they are grounds for proceeding slowly and with caution. Here are some suggestions:

- Explain to the students that, by working in pairs or in groups, they will have more opportunities to use the language, and without the pressure of speaking in front of the whole class and the teacher. Use the students' first language if necessary.
- Begin with pairwork under direct supervision. One way to start is to have students do an exercise individually and then check it with their neighbour. This could be done with Exercise 2 in the first part of Materials extract 6.1, for example.
- Another alternative is to start with an open pair – two students doing an activity in front of the rest of the class before moving to closed pairs, where all the students work in pairs without other students listening. This could be done with Exercise 3 in the first part of Materials extract 6.1, for example. To begin with, the teacher can tell the students very explicitly which twos are to work together, and then say:

Everyone on this side of the pair is Student A. Everyone on the other side is Student B. Student A, you are Sandy. Student B, you are Nina. Now practise the conversation together.

After a while, this amount of instruction can be reduced to: *Please do this exercise in pairs.*

- As students become more used to pairwork, you can move on to a freer approach. Let us take the simple example of practising *how many* with plural nouns using a mingle activity. For example, students can create a simple questionnaire by writing the names of five or ten classmates on a piece of paper. They then stand up and go to those people and collect the relevant information. You can compile a list of nouns to suit your students and their level: with children it might be *brothers and sisters*, with adults it might be *children*. It is the teacher's responsibility to negotiate this in context with the students.

How many _____ do you have?			
Name	**children**	**sons**	**daughters**
Pedro	3	1	2
Clara	0	—	—
Ahmed	1	1	0
Yoko			

Figure 6.5 A sample class questionnaire

If the students are encouraged to write the names of people they do not know well, imagine the effect this simple exercise can have in terms of meaningful practice, real communication, and class rapport.

So far, we have discussed groupwork as though it were the same as pairwork, because it is S↔S interaction. In one important way, however, it is not the same. In pairwork, when one person is silent, the other person is usually called on to speak. In groupwork, it is possible for one student to dominate, or for another to remain silent and let the others carry out the task. Some people talk more than others, and people learn differently, so different proportions of student talk need not be seen as a problem. Nevertheless, the teacher needs to take action if one group member is dominating the interaction when others would like to speak but are not getting the chance. Here are ways you can respond to this situation:

1   In terms of the task itself, make sure that everyone has something to contribute to the whole and make it clear that everyone must cooperate in order to complete the task. Notice in the task in Materials extract 6.2 how students start with a discussion in pairs and then move into groups of four to share their ideas, before coming together to discuss the activity as a class. The contribution of each student to this task could be further increased by mixing the pairs when the students get into groups of four. Instead of A1 and A2 working with B1 and B2, and C1, C2 with D1, D2, you can have A1, B1, C1, D1 working together and A2, B2, C2, D2 working together. That way each member of the original pair will not be able to rely on the original partner to report their discussion.

2   As students get used to groupwork, encourage them to pay attention to how they interact in groups. Say to the class: If you notice that you are talking a lot, or that someone else is not saying much, ask that person, *'What do you think?'*.

3   The more freedom you give your students, the more important it is that they understand exactly what they are supposed to do. So, before the pairwork or groupwork starts:

- ask one of the students to repeat the instructions, or
- have one pair or one group demonstrate the activity to the class.

> **2** Work with a partner. Which of these inventions do you
> think is the most important? Mark them ☐ for the
> most important to ☒ for the least important.
>
> | | |
> |---|---|
> | ☐ the computer | ☐ nuclear weapons |
> | ☐ the car | ☐ the space rocket |
> | ☐ the television | ☐ the mobile phone |
> | ☐ the aeroplane | ☐ the space satellite |
>
> **3** Work in groups of four. Work together to agree on the
> three most important inventions. Which has changed
> the world the most?
>
> **4** Talk together as a class. What other machines,
> inventions, or discoveries would you add to the list?

Materials extract 6.2 Soars and Soars: New Headway Plus Intermediate,
page 12

4 During pairwork and groupwork, you need to be available to help where necessary, but the main part of your job is to move round and listen in order to be able to evaluate progress and eventually give feedback. (See Chapter 7.)

5 Physically speaking, four or five is an ideal size for a group. Six people will probably split up into two subgroups. Also, students need to be actually *in* a group – a line of students is *not* a group, so it is important to get students used to quick and quiet movement.

6 GROUP DYNAMICS are important. If you have a mixed ability class, you should try to vary the groupings so that sometimes you have learners of the same level working together and sometimes you have mixed-level groups, with weaker learners supported by stronger ones.

7 Tasks for pairwork and groupwork should:

- be clearly understood in English
- include input in, and work with, English
- involve some spoken or written outcome in English (in Materials extract 6.2, the groups of four have to agree on the three most important inventions).

8 After pairs or groups have completed their task, you need to be able to get the students' attention back to you again. One way is to have a small bell, for example, to signal you want the class's attention. Another way is to raise your hand; as the students notice you, they stop what they are doing and put their hands up, too. The whole class will quite quickly notice the activity has come to an end, even without a verbal prompt.

As long as the above characteristics of group and pairwork are in place, do not worry too much if students sometimes use their first language.

This last point deserves some discussion in its own right, because we have repeatedly argued for the importance of using English as the language of the classroom, both for teaching and for management purposes.

First language and second language

In classrooms where learners come from different language backgrounds, the teacher has no choice but to communicate somehow in English. In this situation, we have found that even if we do speak the language of some of the students, we prefer not to, as it threatens the unity of the class.

Wherever possible, the class should be conducted in English, including all greetings, taking the register, handing out papers, and so on. If all this is done in English it:

- demonstrates clearly that English is a form of living communication to be *used*, not just a subject to be *studied*
- provides students with extra practice in hearing and using English
- gives students a chance to acquire some language naturally
- introduces forms and uses of the language which the syllabus may not cover.

You can speak simply and clearly, support what you say with gestures, facial expressions, and actions, but insist on running the class in English. At first you may meet resistance and/or giggles, but it is worth persevering because if you can engage your students in this small, English-using community, you have made a most important contribution to their learning. However:

- Do not insist on the use of English if the level of frustration on a particular occasion becomes too high. If the students really cannot understand you, or if a student really cannot express something that he or she clearly very much wants to say, use the first language. Then make a point of showing the class how this is said in English – they will be very ready to learn at this point. If you do not speak the students' first language, encourage the whole class to help out.
- In a monolingual class, use your knowledge of the shared L1 where this can help students to see useful comparisons or contrasts with English. In other words, make the L1 an object of study as you make English the preferred language of communication.
- Try not to be discouraged if the students continue to use their first language among themselves. In a monolingual class, it takes students great dedication to struggle with a second language, when they can so easily say what they want to in their first language. Some teachers use praise, some use threats, others use fines in order to stop use of the L1. The

important thing for you is to do what is appropriate in your teaching context, for the students to know why you are so insistent on the use of English, and for the atmosphere to remain positive, friendly, and good-humoured.

Before we end this section, we can extend a little further the idea of a classroom community. Make every effort to encourage small, everyday exchanges in English. For example:

TEACHER	What d'you do electronic engineering or …?
MARTINO	No, civil… civil engineering
TEACHER	Did you do the exam in English?
MARTINO	Yes. Er is abilitazione abilitation
TEACHER	Yeah, engineering's really …
MARTINO	Ah si – difficult.
TEACHER	How many years have you been …?
MARTINO	Five years.
TEACHER	Five?
MARTINO	Yes

It is necessary to maintain a balance between the desire to communicate and the desire and need to be correct. You might think that the example above is not a good example for a language classroom. The learner's contributions are not correct and neither, perhaps, are the teacher's. But as an informal exchange, it works and achieves its purpose of making English a natural means of intelligible communication.

Finally, with regard to the classroom community, we need to touch on possible problems with unacceptable behaviour. If you do not share the same cultural and linguistic background as your students, try to find out what kind of behaviour they expect in class. Even if you do share their background, remember that if you are introducing new forms of activity, it will not always be clear to students exactly what the rules are or where the changes end.

Questions of conduct are so tied to particular societies that we will treat this subject only from a language teaching angle. Wherever possible, classroom behaviour should be a topic of discussion. At elementary level, it is possible to work at building up a code of conduct in simple English and as a set of rules, for example:

1 Students always do their homework on time.
2 The teacher always returns the homework next lesson.
3 If students come to class late …
4 If the teacher comes to class late …

With more advanced students, it might be possible to start a discussion with:

What kind of	teacher behaviour	is most	helpful	to learning?
	student		harmful	

You could also introduce a learning contract which you negotiate with your students. This would outline their and your duties and responsibilities.

Building a community with shared rules may not solve all discipline problems, but making behaviour an open topic can help prevent problems occurring. And if teachers are consistent in their behaviour and their classes are clearly well prepared, they can expect the support of their English-using community if and when difficulties do arise.

Summary

In this chapter we looked at classroom management from the point of view of managing the planning before a lesson and of managing interactions during a lesson.

The keys to class management are *communication*, *choice*, and *commitment*. Fortunately, they are also the keys to language learning. Work with your students to plan relevant objectives within realistic timescales, and to create a class rapport that is conducive to learning.

Questions and activities

Think about your responses and then discuss them with a colleague if possible.

1 Have you ever used a questionnaire to find out what your students' needs are? Was it useful?
2 Has any teacher ever used a questionnaire with you as a student? Was it useful? How would you respond to the questionnaire on page 88 if you were thinking of learning a new language?
3 In your experience as a learner or teacher, how easy is it to describe objectives in terms of what students will be able to do?
4 Look through some materials, with a specific group of students in mind if possible. How many lessons would you expect to spend on those materials? Alternatively, how much material would you need for a one-hour class? Compare your responses with those of a colleague.
5 Complete the 90-minute lesson plan to achieve and check the objectives stated on page 96.
6 Can you suggest general improvements to the style of our lesson plan? How could you personalize it for your own use? If you are studying for a teaching certificate, how does this plan compare with what is required of you?

7 What interactions did you experience in class as a learner? Which do you use as a teacher? How do individual styles or cultural background affect this?
8 What dangers (if any) do you see in treating the class as a 'social event', as well as a formal lesson? What do you learn from your response?
9 Have you ever treated behaviour in class as a topic for discussion with your students? If so, what was their reaction? If not, what do you think their reaction would be? What would you want to include in a learning contract with your students with regard to their and your duties and responsibilities?

(For answers, thoughts, and comments on these questions, see page 184.)

7 FROM COMMUNICATION TO LANGUAGE

This chapter explores one of the two approaches to language teaching introduced in Chapter 2 and further discussed in the introduction to Part Two,
as we turned our attention to classroom action and teaching procedures. As
with all the chapters of this book, we expect the reader to recognize most
of what is being described from your experience as language learner and/or
teacher. The challenge throughout is to recognize patterns in that experience
and turn experience into knowledge – the kind of knowledge that can then
be used to shape and improve future experience.

The pattern that guides teaching in this chapter is a movement from an
initial concentration on meaning, function, communication, and on getting
something *done*, to a later concentration on language *form* if that proves
necessary. In other words, to take a straightforward example, the teacher will
not approach a lesson with the explicit aim of teaching the present perfect
form of the English verb; this would be to set a goal based on language form.
The teacher might approach a lesson by asking the students to find out from
the rest of the class how many countries they have visited, individually and/
or collectively; this would be to set a non-linguistic goal. The goal would
have linguistic implications in that learners would probably use the present
perfect to complete the task if they engage in it as aware language learners,
but the point is that they have a communicative goal to achieve, using any
language available to them.

The thinking behind this approach is that:

- A vital part of learning a language involves the act of communication
  itself.
- Acts of communication enable people to bring together and integrate for
  real-time use elements of language that they have learned in various ways
  but not previously mastered in such a meaningful way.
- The relative successes, failures, and manoeuvres involved in learner communication enable learners to move forward in their language development.

They also enable learners and teachers to identify what it is that students still need to learn, and are ready to learn.

An overall framework for such goal-oriented activity will ensure that students are called upon to:

- *gather* information in English (from other people, from other sources, or from thinking about their own knowledge, opinions, experiences, etc.)
- *exchange* information (in English, with classmates) and work together in order to
- *produce* information in English (in some kind of text, either spoken or written, that represents the outcome of the task, or perhaps a report on how the task was completed).

As we shall see below, all these stages provide opportunities for focusing on language form, as appropriate, while engaging in goal-oriented activities.

Within this very general framework, many possible types of activity are possible. We are going to start by looking at different types of task in the language classroom and at one particular approach to ELT which uses tasks, rather than language items, as its organizing principle – that is task-based learning. We shall then look at other communicative activities: projects, role-plays, simulations, and games. We will not be describing these as though they were totally separate from each other: it is easy to imagine a project which includes separate tasks, or a role-play within a game.

Our purpose here is to encourage our readers to ask themselves the same questions that recur throughout this book:

- How much of what you read here do you recognize from your own experience?
- What do you know now that you did not know before?
- Can you express what you know any differently?
- How does any of this affect what you might do in the future?

Tasks

In its most fundamental meaning, a task is a communicative activity in which students are given an outcome to achieve beyond just using the language. Tasks are a way of having students do things in English. The most important thing is not that students use the language correctly, but that they complete the task successfully, using whatever linguistic resources at their disposal.

As teachers, we can expect three types of positive effect here. First, students can be intrinsically or extrinsically motivated by the goal that has been set for them. Second, while concentrating on the task and the cooperative work carried out in order to achieve the outcome, students often lose self-consciousness and engage subconsciously with the language in ways that support their overall learning. Third, students are further motivated when they feel a sense of actually having achieved something through their use of English.

Let us look at a simple example in the area of listening comprehension, a topic to which we return in Chapter 9. Can students understand a recorded dialogue? In order to find out, we could ask them questions, which we might think of as a linguistic exercise, or we could set them a task.

In Materials extract 7.1, the students are asked to listen to a recording and the task is to put the pictures in the right order. A simple teaching procedure would be:

1 Tell students to look at the picture story in pairs and try to predict some of the things that happened during the journey. This prepares the students for what they are going to hear in the recording. It also allows them to ask questions about vocabulary. If any questions are raised, see if other students can supply the words before you do so yourself.
2 Play the recording and have students put the pictures in order by writing the numbers in the right place. The fact that the students are being called upon to listen and *do* something is probably already motivating. Notice that their linguistic task so far is to *gather* information. At this level the task remains simple.
3 Tell the students to check their results in pairs. Having gathered information, they *exchange* information with their partners. Although they have listened to the same recording, there may be differences of opinion on what they heard and understood. This then is the basis of their exchange.
4 Ask pairs to volunteer their results. Do not indicate whether you agree or not until all the students have agreed or disagreed and put forward their reasons. Students thus have to *produce* information in the form of a statement of what they saw and what they heard. When you have gathered all the responses, play the recording again to clear up any disagreements.

As we noted in Chapter 6, it may be that some of the information exchange will take place in languages other than English. If this happens despite your best efforts at persuasion, it should not be a problem – at least the information gathering and production are in English. Also, as the students know that they will have to give their responses in English, you can encourage them to use some of the information exchange time to prepare that English.

There is one more point to note here before we move on. We talked about the first part of the task being simple. That is to say, there is a distinction between difficulty of language and difficulty of task. This is important because the two can be balanced. This, in turn, means that learners at elementary level can

2 LISTENING

a   (2.12) Listen to Martin talking about his journey from
    London to Avignon by car. Number the pictures 1–7.

b   Listen again. Mark the sentences T (true) or F (false).

    1 There's a lot of traffic in London on Saturday mornings.
    2 Petrol is more expensive in Britain than in France.
    3 There are two ways to cross the English Channel by car.
    4 You can't drive through the Channel Tunnel.
    5 The journey through the tunnel takes an hour.
    6 Drivers must sit in their car when they go through the tunnel.
    7 The speed limit on French motorways is 120 km/h.
    8 French motorways aren't free.
    9 It's 970 kilometres from Calais to Avignon.

c   (2.13) Listen to Martin talking about his journey and fill in the **By car**
    column in the chart. Now compare the information with your answers in 1a.

London to Avignon	By plane	By train	By car
How long did it take? (from home)	5 hours 45 mins	6 hours 40 mins	
How much did it cost?	£63	£65.80	
Comfort /10	5	8	
Convenience /10	5	9	

d   Think of a town / city in your country. How many different ways are
    there of getting there? Which do you think is the best? Why?

*Materials extract 7.1   Oxenden and Latham-Koenig: English File
Intermediate, page 29*

be motivated by having authentic materials to work with (see Chapter 4), as long as they are given simple tasks to do.

Different types of task

A common type of task in ELT is one in which students are given different information which they need to communicate to each other in order to complete a task. For example, you can cut up a picture story and give a different picture, or pictures, to each student in a group. The students then have to tell the others in their group about their picture or pictures. In order to tell the story, the group has to decide how to order the pictures correctly. These are called information gap activities.

When students are asked to read or listen to different texts and then share information to complete a task, this is often referred to as jigsaw listening or reading, because of the need to fit the various pieces together. Materials extract 7.2 is an example of a jigsaw listening task.

While so far we have spoken about information gaps, the same kind of work can be done on the basis of opinion gaps. The opinions concerned may be the learners' own, or opinions given in the materials. If the latter is the case, the activity becomes more like a role-play. We shall be returning to this later.

There are many different task-types. (See Willis and Willis, 2007.) Some of the most common ones are:

LISTENING AND SPEAKING
The reunion

1 Three friends, Alan, Sarah, and James, were all at university together in Durham, a town in the north of England. Now, ten years later, they are planning a reunion. Divide into two groups.

Group A
[T 5.10] Listen to Alan phoning Sarah.

Group B
[T 5.11] Listen to Sarah phoning James.

Listen and complete as much as possible of the chart. The following names are mentioned.

Claypath   the Lotus Garden   the Midlands
The County   The Three Tuns   Leeds
the Kwai Lam   Saddler Street   Sunderland

2 Check your answers with people in your group.

	Alan	Sarah	James
Travelling from?			
How?			
Leaving at what time?			
Arriving in Durham at?			
Staying where?			
Going to which restaurant?			
Where is it?			
Where are they going to meet?			
What time?			

3 Find a partner from the other group. Swap information to complete the chart.

4 What might go wrong with their arrangements? Or will everything work out all right? Who's meeting who where?

Materials extract 7.2 Soars and Soars: New Headway Upper-Intermediate, page 52

- *Ordering* and *sequencing*. Students put materials into some sort of order. These may be jumbled paragraphs, pictures, or sentences. Exercise 7.1 is an example of a sequencing task.
- *Matching*. Students are asked to match pairs of items. For example, they might be asked to join two halves of an expression or a sentence, or label a picture with the correct words from a list.
- *Categorizing*. Students have to sort items into groups. They might be given lists of kinds of food (for example, pomegranates, chicken, broccoli) and asked to sort them into fruit, meat, and vegetables. Alternatively, they are not given the categories and are asked to decide on their own categories. This is perhaps more motivating and more challenging as students can be asked to justify their choices.
- *Prioritizing* or *rank ordering*. Students have to select the most important things in a given situation or put things in order of importance. Materials extract 6.2 (see page 101) is an example of a ranking task, where students are asked to put inventions in order of importance.
- *Problem solving*. Students work together to solve a problem.

If students have been asked to communicate in order to complete a task, they must be left to get on with it. At the same time, the teacher should be available to answer any questions that come up – there is no better time for learning than this. The challenge for the teacher is to answer *only* what is asked and no more.

Once the task has been completed, the teacher can focus on any language points he or she wishes to draw attention to. This is often called FOCUS ON FORM. We say more about this in the next section.

So far in this chapter we have looked at tasks as individual events in a lesson. We have noted that such tasks have a non-linguistic outcome. However, it should be clear that such activities can be designed to *encourage* learners to use certain language items that the teacher wants to focus on. So, for example, in completing Materials extract 7.2, the teacher might expect the students to use the present continuous, and the students may well do so as they search their linguistic resources for the best way to express their meanings. The most important thing is that it should not become a problem if they do not. If the teacher insists that students use certain linguistic items to complete a task, the purpose of moving from communication to language is lost, because the underlying belief in this approach is that it is the act of communication itself that is central to language learning.

Task-based learning

The use of tasks in teaching can be formalized into an organized set of procedures, called task-based learning (TBL) or task-based teaching (TBT). Willis and Willis (2007) explains in detail the basis of TBL, along the lines of the principles outlined above:

1 Learners learn a language by using it, hearing it, and seeing it as much as possible.
2 The teacher's job is to provide opportunities for learners to use language in a meaningful way.
3 The teacher should not control the language that is used to complete the task, but should help learners to express their meanings.
4 Once the task is complete, attention given to specific linguistic items that have arisen from the task is useful in promoting language learning.

The teacher may prepare the students before they actually do the task by asking them to do some kind of pre-task. This can have the function of PRE-TEACHING vocabulary, introducing the topic of the task, giving them some initial ideas, or generating interest. As we said above, once students have carried out the task, the teacher may decide to focus on a particular aspect of the language and this is called focus on form. Focus on form often consists of consciousness-raising activities based on language awareness, and is designed to draw students' attention to how they actually used language in the task. In this approach, students may be given practice activities too, but these are not central.

Let us look at what a TBL lesson might look like by structuring a lesson around the task in Materials extract 6.2:

1 Students are given a list of the names of the inventions, together with a picture of each one. They have to match the names and the pictures. This acts as a pre-task by *presenting* the vocabulary the students need for the main task. It is also a *matching* task in its own right. Students can be asked to compare their answers in pairs, before being given feedback by the teacher.
2 In pairs, students have to agree on the rank ordering of the inventions. This is one of the main tasks and in this phase the teacher should just listen and not intervene unless the students ask for help. The fact that students have to reach an agreement is likely to lead to a lot of discussion.
3 The teacher puts each pair with another pair to compare their answers and to decide on the three most important inventions and the one that has most changed the world. This constitutes a second task. The teacher's role is the same as in the previous stage of the lesson.
4 The teacher asks each group of four which invention they think has most changed the world and why. This is sometimes called the *report* phase. As students have completed their task and are now reporting on what they have already decided, it is likely that the language they use will be more accurate as they will pay more attention to it. Students can be asked to keep a record of which inventions are nominated. This gives them a reason

to listen to the other groups and also means they can provide the information if asked.

5   Students listen to a recording of competent English speakers doing the same task and find out if they reached the same decisions or not. Even if such recordings do not exist in the coursebook, it is relatively easy to record competent English speakers doing the same task as the students. This extends the task by giving students a model of language as well as giving them practice in listening to unscripted spoken English. A TRANSCRIPT of the recording can then be used as the basis for focus on form activities.

6   Students are asked to identify features of the language in the transcript. Drawing students' attention to the way the language is used in spontaneous spoken English will help them to become aware of features of the language that they may not come across in published materials, but which they will certainly meet outside the classroom. For example, the focus could be on the use of discourse markers, such as *well, right, OK,* and so on. Such language awareness activities can also be followed by another task, such as 'Underline all the expressions of agreement and disagreement in the text. Which express the strongest agreement/disagreement? Which the mildest?'

7   Students may be asked to practise particular language points. If the teacher feels it useful or appropriate, supplementary practice exercises can be introduced at this stage to give students controlled practice of specific language items. (See Chapter 8.)

The above is based on the task cycle described in Willis (1996). This is not the only version of TBL and not all TBL lessons would involve all these stages. Steps 5 and 6, for example, will not fit every task or indeed be possible in all contexts.

Other communicative activities

Projects

We have seen how tasks can become more and more complex in terms of what students are asked to do as they *gather, exchange,* and *produce* information. All the information in the above examples was provided in the classroom materials themselves. It is possible, however, to have students gather information from the outside world. When relatively large-scale activities are set up, using authentic information, these activities are often called PROJECT WORK. (See Chapter 9, Materials extract 9.2.)

Projects are the kind of large-scale activity that teachers can develop in their own situations. What issues concern people where you live? What we hope results from projects is depth of personal involvement in meaningful experience. This will certainly further learning.

For example, a group of European business people studying in England might be interested in the issue of heavy penalties for the use of mobile phones while driving. Some of them might use their phone while driving, some might not. Some will be in favour of heavy penalties, and some will be against. They can devise a project to gather together different points of view on this issue. Here are some guidelines the teacher might follow, although not all of them will be relevant in every situation.

1 Make sure that carrying out the project is not going to annoy or upset anyone, either inside or outside the school.
2 Write down in negotiation with the students a clear statement of the purpose(s) of the project which everyone understands. The purpose might also include oral presentations of the findings to the rest of the group and a written record of the collected findings. Here the main purpose of the project might be to gather different points of view on the question:
   Should the use of mobile phones while driving carry such heavy penalties?
3 Check that everyone understands their responsibilities at each stage. On this project, one group of students could go to the local police station, another could read newspaper and magazine articles, and a third could go to a large car park to interview motorists. Such sources of information can be decided on in class discussion.
4 Make sure you have made personal contacts where necessary and that your students are expected and will be welcomed wherever they are going.
5 Allow plenty of time. Do not get involved in anything but the smallest projects unless you are prepared to give up your own time. When students get involved in processing real information, they can become very serious indeed about doing things properly and doing them well, and this takes time.
6 Keep your projected outcomes simple. This is connected with the last point. For example, oral presentations and written reports can consist simply of a brief scene-setting and a list of opinions, plus reasons given.

Any written outcomes could later be presented to the school for use as possible discussion material with other classes.

Projects can be used as part of TBL. They are also the basis of project-based learning (PBL), which, as the name suggests, is another formalization of generally available ideas based on projects that the students have to complete. In PBL, a whole course can be based on one big project and it is often used in teaching English for Specific Purposes. For example, students of business English might be asked to set up an imaginary company and develop a business plan for it. Or students of engineering might be asked to design a particular project, carrying out all the necessary steps as if it were an actual undertaking.

Role-plays and simulations

At its simplest, role-play is built into ELT from the earliest stages, when students are asked to say the lines of a dialogue. If teachers keep this in mind, better use can be made of dialogues by not letting students simply read each line aloud. When students are speaking a dialogue, they should look at the person they are addressing, and speak their lines meaningfully. In other words, students should *speak* dialogues, not *read* them.

As we noted in Chapter 3, we can extend this idea to speaking lines in exercises as well. The functional conversation exercise we looked at in Materials extract 3.4 is also a kind of role-play, even though the students are given a lot of what they have to say.

A further extension of this is when students are given role cards containing information about the person whose part they are going to act. Materials extract 7.3 is an example.

Here, the materials provide an outcome to be achieved (finding things in common) in order to produce a situation where communication is necessary. But role-play is obviously not simply another information-gap activity. The main difference is the element of pretence. What we really hope to gain from role-play is that learners can *play-act*. Instead of struggling to say what they mean, they can pretend to mean what they say.

At its best, this means that they can forget about having to take responsibility for the opinions they express. So, allow time to talk through the purpose of role-plays and encourage participants to gather ideas about how to play at being different characters and to play with the language.

At the same time, some students will be uncomfortable doing this type of activity. With them, explain that this is not a form of theatre – they will not be asked to perform for anyone else, unless they wish to. The other point to make is that a role-play can always be used as a simple practice activity if that is the limited investment that students are prepared to make.

Like role-plays, *simulations* involve pretence. In simulations, however, students are not so much asked to play at being someone else. They are rather asked to be themselves in an imaginary situation. Thus the basis of simulation is not given dialogues, but the type of activity seen in Materials extract 7.4.

What is usually meant by simulation is an activity in which each participant is given background information, and is then expected to use his or her own skills and values in order to take part. Materials extract 7.5, for example, is a small-scale simulation in a business situation, in which we assume the learners have already been given the necessary information.

ABC Put it all together

15 Work with a partner. Look at the **Flight to Athens** role cards on » p.131. Each choose a different role card. Read your role card and write a few words to help you remember the main information.

16 Do a role play. Imagine you are on a flight to Athens together. Start a conversation. What have you got in common?

10C Put it all together
Flight to Athens

Role card 1 Erik / Erika
You're travelling for work. You're a tour guide and you work for a company called *Sun Tours*. You've worked for them since 2007. Before that, you worked for *Golden Holidays*. You've been a tour guide for seven years. You're from Denmark, but you've lived in Brussels, Belgium, since 2001. You enjoy painting and reading detective novels. Your boyfriend / girlfriend is from Manchester, in England.

Role card 2 Manuel / Manuela
You're Mexican and you're on holiday in Europe. You've been in Europe since April. You've visited Britain and Belgium. You're going to tour Greece with a company called *Golden Holidays*. You've lived in Houston, Texas, in the USA, since 2002. You've been a full-time writer for five years. You write detective novels. You're married and your wife / husband works for a company called *Techno-Sonic*.

Role card 3 Josef / Josefina
You're travelling for work. You're a translator and you're travelling with a group of tourists from Prague in the Czech Republic. The group is going to tour Greece with a company called *Golden Holidays*. You've been a translator since you left university in 2004. You've lived in Prague since 1999. You speak Czech, Greek, English, and Italian. Sometimes you work at the European Union in Brussels.

Role card 3 Justin / Justine
You're on holiday with a tour company called *Sun Tours*. You're from Manchester but you've lived in London for six years. You work for a company called *Techno-Sonic*. The company makes intercom systems. You've worked there since 2003. You often travel for work – last year you went to Brussels, Copenhagen, and Houston. You're married. Your husband / wife is from Prague, in the Czech Republic.

Materials extract 7.3   Hancock and McDonald: English Result Pre-Intermediate, pages 101 and 131

Simulations are often used on ESP courses to motivate learners by putting them in scenarios similar to their own work situations.

4B What would you do if…? **Student A**

a Ask B your questions. Put the verbs in brackets in the past simple.

What would you do if you…?
(meet) your English teacher at a party
(find) a lot of extra money in your bank account
(get) a present from your partner that you really didn't like
(hit) somebody's car in a car park
(have) to sing at a karaoke evening
(be) invited to a really good concert by somebody you didn't like
(see) your best friend's personal diary open on a table

b Answer B's questions. Ask *What about you?*

Materials extract 7.4 Oxenden and Latham-Koenig: New English File Intermediate, page 117

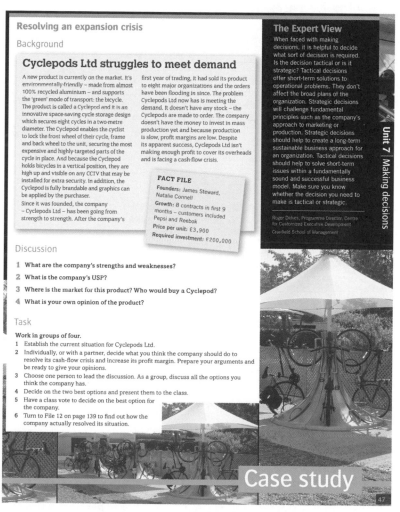

Materials extract 7.5 Duckworth and Turner: Business Result Upper-Intermediate, page 47

When setting up a role-play or simulation, the most important things to do are:

1 Make sure that everyone understands the purpose and their own part in the activity. It is often useful in a class where the same role-play will be carried out by a number of groups, to begin by getting together all the players of each role and having them discuss what they understand by the role description and how they intend to act it out.
2 Be available but not involved, unless you are needed to keep the activity going.
3 Monitor language use and make notes on student needs.
4 Allow time afterwards for students to talk about what happened. This will raise general awareness of what can happen in role-plays and simulations. It can help students to learn from uncomfortable situations that may have arisen. It may also perhaps encourage them to become more involved next time. This sharing is important because it is otherwise difficult to provide in the ELT class a common experience emerging from such widely differing individual experiences.
5 Introduce a language focus. This can be based both on student questions and on notes you have made.
6 Allow plenty of time!

Games

What words do you think of when you see the word *game?* We hope that your responses include such words as *play, fun, cooperation,* and *competition.* The aims common to all communicative activities – to have people relaxed and enjoying themselves, acquiring language through natural use, as well as making learnt language more readily available – are particularly important here.

When teaching young children, this type of approach is especially relevant, but relaxation and enjoyment are important to all learners, and the most serious of adults can become completely absorbed in cooperating with colleagues in order to win a game. Here is a simple game involving the use of the present continuous to describe current action:

1 Write a list of actions on a piece of paper (for example, eating spaghetti, typing on the computer, and so on).
2 Call one student to the front and show him or her one action on your list.
3 The student mimes the action.
4 Classmates raise their hands if they want to speak.
5 The teacher (or possibly the student) nominates someone, who is allowed one guess, to answer, for example: *You're opening a bottle.*
6 The student miming responds: *No, I'm not/Yes, I am.*

To turn this into a competition, divide the class into two halves, one facing the front and one facing the back. A student from each group comes to you for the first word. This student then mimes the action in front of his or her group. As soon as it has been guessed, another student comes for the next word. The game ends when one team gets to the end of your list, or when everyone in the group has had a turn. You appoint an observer for each group to make sure that everyone is playing fairly and that the required language is produced on each occasion.

Games can also be used for individual work, pair work, or small group work. Materials extract 7.6, for example, is a 'Spot the difference game' carried out in pairs:

6C   They're having a party!   **Student A**

You and **B** have the same picture but with eight differences.

a   Tell **B** what is happening in the **left** side of your picture. **B** will tell you what is different in his / her picture. Circle the differences.

b   Listen to **B** telling you what is happening in the **right** side of his / her picture. Look at your picture. Tell **B** the differences. Circle them on your picture.

c   When you've finished, compare the two pictures.

Materials extract 7.6 Oxenden, Latham-Koenig, and Seligson: New English File Elementary, page 110

This game encourages cooperation in pairs, but also introduces a competitive element between teams, and this generally increases motivation to see which pair finishes first. An activity such as this can also be given to pairs who finish other work early. Finally, in the same way that games can be useful for older learners as well as young, they can also have their uses at any level of language learning, so long as they help to maintain a relaxed atmosphere and help learners engage meaningfully with the language.

Other communication-based methods

TBL and PBL are not the only approaches to ELT that are based on a principle of communication first. Content Based Learning, also known as Content and Language Integrated Learning (CLIL) is becoming increasingly popular.

In CLIL students learn other subjects, such as maths or history, through the medium of a language that is not their first language. CLIL is well established in immersion programmes in Canada, for example, but the globalization of English we discussed in Chapter 3 has also meant that English is increasingly used as the language of instruction where it is not traditionally a second language. This is the case of some schools and universities in Turkey, for instance.

Activity-based learning is a more general term that refers to any method based on learning the language through doing activities that involve physical movement and engagement. This type of approach is often used with young learners, who learn better through doing, rather than through explicit language teaching.

Summary

In this chapter we have looked at both the principles and methods underlying one of the two fundamental approaches to teaching English discussed in this and the next chapter. We have looked at various types of communicative activity: tasks, projects, role-plays, simulations, and games, which generally involve gathering, exchanging, and producing information in English. Such activities are useful because they motivate learners, they further the learning process itself, they give the teacher information on progress, and they thereby provide a context for deciding which elements of language form the learners need help with. We have also seen how the basic principles involved can be formalized into approaches that have their own specific names.

We hope we have given you a clear picture of what we mean by *moving from communication to language*. It is now time to look at the principles and methods underlying the other fundamental approach, *moving from language to communication*, and that is the focus of the next chapter.

Questions and activities

Think about your responses and then discuss them with a colleague if possible.

1 What experience do you have of communicative activities, either as a learner or as a teacher? In what ways do these experiences lead you to agree or disagree with points made in the chapter?
2 Tasks and other activities are always referred to as *meaningful*, which is easy to say, harder to do. How might one try to ensure that such work is actually meaningful to the learners?
3 If you wanted to use recordings of 'competent speakers of English' carrying out tasks, as suggested in the chapter, who might you record? Can you foresee any difficulties arising from whichever example or model you choose?

4 Can you think of a local project for your teaching situation? You need a question to answer, or a problem to respond to, and different sources of information to draw on. Which students would this be suitable for?

5 Do you find 'play-acting' a useful way to help you relax about what you say, or does it make you feel nervous? Might it be helpful if you had the chance to get used to it? Are your feelings common in your context? Are you sure?

6 Look at the role-play and simulation materials. Write step-by-step procedures for using them, similar to the one given for the lesson plan in Materials extract 6.1 on page 96.

7 What games do you know which could be useful for language learning?

(For answers, thoughts, and comments on these questions, see page 185.)

8 FROM LANGUAGE TO COMMUNICATION

We talked in Chapter 1 about the importance of creating a safe, English-using environment in which students feel encouraged to express themselves. In Chapter 7, we saw how this can be achieved by emphasizing the importance of non-linguistic goals, in order to reduce pressure on the learners to be formally accurate in their use of language until they have achieved that goal.

In this chapter, we make the complementary (and *not* alternative) suggestion that a safe environment can also be created by taking the pressure off students to achieve non-linguistic goals until they have a clear idea of how the language they are trying to learn takes form.

So, driving the approach that we take up in this chapter are three principles:

1 A vital part of learning a language is having a working understanding of how the language forms its meanings.
2 A focus on linguistic objectives in systematic ways allows learners to develop a clear idea of what it is they are learning and how well they are learning it.
3 The acquisition of discrete parts of the language in meaningful ways allows learners to build a cognitive framework for further learning and gives them the confidence to use the language in communication.

In order to teach from *language* to *communication*, then, it is necessary to break the language down into small units, taught one at a time in the context of what has been previously learnt. Learners gradually put the 'bits' together to build up a scaffolding for their learning of the language as a whole. In principle, the language items introduced can be selected on the basis of any of the perspectives on language description that we looked at in Chapter 3.

In terms of teaching procedure, the general approach by the teacher is as follows:

- introduce meaningful models of the language item(s) the students need
- conduct careful practice of the language presented

- organize communicative interaction
- give feedback on the students' use of the language.

There is a commonsense sequence here: students are shown something new, practise it, have the opportunity to use it meaningfully, and then they find out from the teacher how they are getting on. We also saw this sequence in Chapter 4, when we talked about a possible move from published materials to local materials. But note that these are not fixed stages of a lesson nor even a simple sequence of events. The points above constitute a list of steps all interconnected with each other. A capable teacher is always sensitive to ways of conducting useful feedback, ready at all times to encourage meaningful communication, never averse to providing an opportunity to practise, and constantly aware that he or she is a model of language use. As we did in Chapter 2, however, we shall separate these ideas out in order to be able to make them clear. As we discuss the points, we shall exemplify them with teaching materials, beginning with the materials we used in the lesson plan in Chapter 6. Please refer back to those materials in the course of reading this chapter.

There is a teaching decision involved here. We could have used different examples from different books. This would have introduced a wider range of materials. We are reusing one extract in the hope of showing more clearly how lesson plans, materials, and methods interconnect. This kind of decision is central to methodology: when you decide to do one thing rather than another, you gain something and you lose something.

One final point on this: please remember that we are *not* suggesting that we should teach English only by following a coursebook. We are using sample materials to help us discuss teaching procedures. We use the procedures to help us talk about underlying principles. Your task is then to relate these principles to procedures and materials appropriate in your own situation.

Introducing meaningful models of language

It is easy, but mistaken, to think of the introduction of new language as the beginning of a lesson. The teaching procedure should begin before that introduction if the learning is going to be successful. We mentioned in Chapter 6 the importance of:

- an introductory warm-up activity to get the class under way
- a review of something learnt earlier which is particularly relevant to what is coming (introducing something new in the context of something already known should be a regular feature of teaching).

Furthermore, as well as being sure about the relevance of the language to the students as learners, the teacher also has to be sure that it is relevant to them as people. These issues are clearly not separate. Let us return to Materials extract 6.1.

It is clear from the lesson plan on page 96 what the immediate aims and objectives are. We can answer the questions about the relevance of the new language as follows:

- It is relevant to the students as learners because it is a logical next step in helping them master the form and use of questions with *like*.
- It is relevant to the students as people, because it will enable a group of individuals to communicate appropriately with each other and about each other. This will give them authentic social practice and encourage cooperation within the group.

So, let us enter the lesson at the point after the local greetings and warmer have taken place:

1 *Test your grammar 1* asks students to complete sentences to test what they already know about the verb patterns that are the focus of the unit.
2 *Test your grammar 2* invites students to give their answers to the class. This enables the teacher to see where the main problems (if any) occur and if he or she has anticipated them accurately on the lesson plan.
3 *Questions with 'like' 1* acts as a lead-in to the topic of the unit. The teacher asks students if they know anyone who has studied abroad. Students can also be asked what they liked/didn't like about the experience. If the students are themselves studying abroad, they can talk about their own experiences.

So topics, vocabulary, structures, and functions from earlier lessons have been reactivated. In this instance, the published materials have covered this stage of the teaching. On other occasions, you will have to take more responsibility for this yourself. We discussed ways of doing this in Chapters 4 and 6.

New language can be provided by the teacher or by the materials, or it can be ELICITED from the students. This last possibility is worth exploring in its own right.

Elicitation

Learning and teaching begin at the edge of what the students already know. So, before you 'teach' something, find out if your students already know it.

The *Test your grammar* part of the materials above is clearly aimed at finding out how much students already know. So, if the response to the prompt *I like my coffee*… is something like *being sweet then the teacher can tell that the verb pattern needs to be presented carefully. If there are lots of responses such as *black with no sugar* the teacher knows not to spend a lot of time on presentation; the lesson can proceed at a brisk pace and language models can be elicited from the students.

Most learners will probably be somewhere in between those two extremes. The point is that the teacher needs to know where they are. Students should be encouraged to show what they know, or think they know. It needs to be made clear that their attempts will be accepted without correction at this stage. This helps the teacher to determine where teaching can usefully begin. Later, students can check what they have learnt against what they thought they knew before.

Another important use of elicitation is when a student asks a question and you turn this question back to the class:

STUDENT: Do we say, 'When they had sung the song', or 'When they had sang the song?

TEACHER: Would anyone like to answer that? Let's see what other people think.

Be careful in cases like this not to hurt anyone's feelings. Explain that the idea is to:

- show that students can learn from each other
- to encourage a feeling of working together
- to take the threat out of being corrected by a colleague.

If you can encourage a caring and cooperative atmosphere, you have gone a long way towards enabling students to work and learn in groups without your constant presence.

Presentation

New language items need to be presented meaningfully, in some kind of communicative context, in a way which will make their use clear. This may be through a situational presentation in which the teacher introduces the new language in a specific situation or through a story, often using pictures or other aids to illustrate meaning. Alternatively, the language can be contextualized first in a written text or a dialogue. Students can be involved in a form of interaction, either by practising the dialogue in pairs, or by looking for information in the text. They may thus get a feel for how the language is used, as well as an understanding of how the new language is formed.

Let us look at what happens in the materials in Materials extract 6.1:

1   *Questions with 'like' 2* presents the target structures in a dialogue. First, students are asked to read the conversation and fill in the questions. They can then check their answers in pairs before they listen for the right answers. Finally, they are asked to practise the conversation in pairs to focus on both the form and the intonation of the questions.

2 *Grammar Spot* checks that students have understood the meaning of the different questions with a matching task. It also draws on metaconscious learning (see Chapter 2) as they are asked to distinguish between *like* as a verb and as a preposition.

3 *Practice 1* gives students the opportunity to practise using the target language in a controlled way. While students are doing the exercise in pairs, the teacher walks round listening to check students have understood and are using the target language accurately. If they are not, then some extra presentation or practice might be necessary.

4 *Practice 2* is a listening exercise that gives further controlled practice as students are asked to distinguish between questions that often cause some confusion.

So, a new item has been meaningfully introduced and clarified. In this instance, we have followed the procedure of presentation and explanation with reference to materials in a coursebook. It should be clear, however, that it is the principles behind the procedure that are important. It is the teacher's responsibility to make sure that new words, structures, and functions are meaningfully presented and properly understood by students. Sometimes, this will involve explicit explanation, to which we now turn.

Explanation

It is impossible to predict exactly which parts of a presentation will be unclear to which students. We do know, however, that some learners need to understand new information (especially grammar) explicitly and appreciate rules of some kind. Ellis (2006) and Lightbown and Spada (2006) for example, review research showing that, while learners might acquire language simply through using it, they tend to learn more quickly if explicit grammar teaching is appropriately included as a part of their learning experience.

There are, consequently, two demands on teachers:

1 to continue to improve their own understanding of the language systems (lexis, grammar, functions, discourse, phonology) they are teaching

2 to use their increasing knowledge to make their explanations shorter, simpler, and more relevant.

For example, a student looking at *Questions with 'like' 2* above might say:

Sometimes, I think, we say, 'What would she like doing at the weekend?', no?

The teacher has access to a variety of possible responses. Let us look at some possibilities:

1 No.

2 No. Why not?

3 No, the verb pattern is 'would like' plus the infinitive.
4 I like the 'at the weekend', but it's What would she like 'to do' at the weekend?, not 'doing'.
5 No, we use 'like doing' to ask and talk about things that we do regularly. Here we are asking what she would like to do on this particular occasion.

You might like to think about your own reactions to those responses before you read our comments.

1 This might sound too blunt and direct, but, in fact, it depends. Some teachers encourage their students to ask as many questions as they like, and they explain to the students that they will always give the shortest answer they can. If that answer is enough, fine. If it is not, ask another question. Perhaps this student can now put this possibility out of mind and get on with learning the correct form. No one else in the class had this problem, so no one's time is wasted. Notice how this type of response depends on teacher and students sharing an understanding of how they work together. This raises another issue: teachers must be careful only to explain things because *their students* need to know them not because *they* know them.
2 The teacher's question can be addressed to an individual student or to the whole class. Here, the teacher has decided that some kind of explanation would be helpful. By eliciting it, the teacher hopes to check the class's general understanding of the rule. Basing these exchanges as far as possible on the words that students choose to use helps to establish common terms for talking about language.
3 The teacher believes that the class understands the grammatical terminology necessary for a brief statement of the rule and that for this student, in this situation, it is more efficient for the teacher to state it. Notice, however, that although the teacher has stated the rule satisfactorily, he or she has not discovered why the student made that mistake in the first place or how effective this explanation has been. This is another example of the point that we made on page 124 above about how methodological choices often involve gaining something and losing something. This option is more efficient in terms of time; the previous option may be more effective in terms of teaching and learning.
4 The teacher welcomes and repeats the new expression, which fits into the lesson. Notice that the teacher then repeats the correct form, not the incorrect one. The teacher also takes care not to give a false impression of the stress in the sentence by over-emphasizing 'to do' when saying...: *It's 'What would she like to do at the weekend', not 'doing'*. An unnatural stress might confuse students when they move on to the pronunciation exercises. In this example, there is no grammatical explanation. Perhaps the teacher wants simply to re-affirm the use of *to do* and contrast this with *doing* later in the lesson.

5 The teacher has decided that the student should be reminded of the common function of the form that is being practised here. Establishing this simple link will be most useful for the learner.

To recapitulate, the teacher needs to build up with each class an agreed way of talking about English and of asking and answering questions about what is being learnt. Some students will have a background of linguistic terminology and some will not. Sometimes it may be necessary to use the students' first language to explain a grammatical point clearly.

Rather than explain rules to students, the teacher may prefer to help the students work the rules out for themselves through guided discovery. The teacher presents examples of the new language and then helps the students to use the examples to work out the rules. This is a form of inductive learning. (See Chapter 2.)

It is also important to check that students have understood the explanations they have been given, either by the teacher or by the coursebook. One way of doing this is by CONCEPT CHECKING. For example, if we want to check that students have understood the meaning of *must have* in a sentence like *Soon Hee must have had a good weekend with Nina and Sandy*, we could ask concept questions such as:

Do you know that she had a good weekend?

Are you fairly sure that she had a good weekend?

Has the weekend finished or not?

For many learners, feelings of security come from understanding how new language works and how it is used. Based on this understanding, students can go on to develop their own skills in using the language.

Conducting careful practice of the language

The purpose of practice is to help students develop what they know *about* the language into an ability to *use* the language. Effective practice guides, verifies, and corrects what the students are producing. It also does some of the following. It:

- focuses on the students' own lives and experiences where possible, in order to deepen the potential learning experience by making the practice personally memorable (See Chapter 1.)
- encourages interaction between students (See Chapter 6.)
- practises the different language skills of speaking, listening, reading, and writing in relation to new items (See Chapter 9.)
- integrates the skills by using a listening or reading passage to provide information for practice activities and/or to work as a model for a speaking or writing exercise. (See Chapter 9.)

In the last section, we left the lesson at a point where the students were practising the new language in a controlled way. Let us return to those materials and look at this practice in more detail.

1   *Practice 1* focuses on the students' own lives and personalizes the language. It also involves students in exchanging personal information, a common social activity. Before students start the activity, you might want to give them some time to think about their answers individually, or even to write something down if you think some might be hesitant to speak. You could also nominate students to give you some sample answers to make sure that everyone knows what to do.

2   *Practice 2* is based on a listening exercise. If students have had any difficulties with the language point, you could first ask them in pairs to predict possible answers to each question. This checks they understand differences in meaning and prepares them for the listening. Once they have listened, they could check their answers in pairs before you nominate students to give the answers to the class. You might also want to extend the exercise and reinforce the new language by asking students some of the questions.

As students work to make their *understanding* of the language point available for *use* through practice activities, teachers will encourage as much communication as possible. We saw an example of such practice activities in Materials extract 4.1.

Organizing communicative interaction

We have already discussed the importance of communication in ELT. (See Chapters 2 and 7.) The main point of relevance here is that when moving from language to communication, there have to be opportunities in the ELT classroom for communicative use of the language being learnt and practised. Let us look once more at the materials in Materials extract 6.1.

1   *Test your Grammar* already involves communicative interaction. The speaker has true, personal, and unpredictable information to communicate to the rest of the class.

2   *Practice 1* involves careful practice of the new language, which also enables the students to take part in communication. In this exercise, the students are asking for and giving real information about themselves. The teacher has control of structure and function, the students have complete freedom of content. This activity can be extended so that each member of the pair writes down one interesting thing that they have learnt about their partner and reports back to the rest of the class. This is an enjoyable follow-up activity; students say what they have found out and have their statements checked, not just for linguistic correctness, but for factual truth (it also guarantees *real* listening). And all the time, exchanges such as these help to strengthen the rapport among the group members.

TEACHER:	Right, José, what did you find out about Nora?
JOSÉ:	Nora likes reading romantic novels.
TEACHER:	Who thinks that's true? Please put your hands up. OK, who thinks it's not? Right. Who doesn't know? OK, Nora, is it true?
NORA:	Yes, it's true. (Or, No! It's not true. I like reading detective stories!)

At this point, we will move away from Materials extract 6.1, as any one set of materials can exemplify only so much.

On other occasions, the teacher also needs to organize communication in a looser way, by providing a context for the use of language, but without directly telling the students what to say. We can see this in Materials extract 2.5.

Look again at the communicative needs of a foreign language learner (see Chapter 2), and notice how the students' backgrounds and feelings are being involved here. Different ideas will produce different exchanges. It is clear how students could use the recently taught language items (*–ing* versus *infinitive*), but they are not instructed to. There is a paradox here at the heart of an approach to language teaching which emphasizes the importance of communication. In real communication, speakers choose freely the forms they use. With a free choice of forms, students may not use what the teacher thinks they should learn and be using.

Successful learners are likely to be those who take the opportunity to use new language forms in the freer, communicative activities that are offered. The teacher's job includes making sure that learners see the connections between practice exercises and communicative activities. We have already suggested having a pair or group model an activity at the beginning of the class to make sure everyone understands exactly what to do. This is also a good time to make sure that students are aware of the linguistic opportunities before them.

During a communicative activity, the teacher's main tasks are to:

- make sure as quickly as possible that everyone has understood what they are supposed to be doing and that they are doing it
- be available in case problems arise
- move round the class and listen carefully in order to monitor language the students are using
- avoid interfering.

This last task is often very difficult. Some teachers find it very nearly impossible not to be the centre of attention; others feel that they are not doing their job unless they are correcting, suggesting, explaining, or somehow demonstrating their presence. But there is plenty for the teacher to do carrying out the first three tasks above, although often this may not look like traditional teaching. But at some stage, if the learners are to have the space to learn, the teacher has to get out of the way.

This is how we try to turn language *practice* into language *use*. The more advanced the students, and the more responsibly they are able to behave, the more complex the activities can become. We have already seen examples of these activities in Chapter 7.

Ways of teaching from language to communication

In Chapter 2, we said that probably the name by which this approach is best known in ELT is Presentation, Practice, Production (PPP). In PPP, new language is first of all presented, either through a dialogue or through a situation, as we showed above. Then students are given the opportunity to practise the new language in a controlled way. Activities at this stage are usually designed so that the students have to use the target language. Finally, the students are given freer practice activities and are strongly encouraged to use the target language, but they may also use other language. Elements of the PPP approach can clearly be seen in Materials extract 6.1. An alternative way is to Test-Teach-Test. Here (and this is reminiscent of a task-based approach) the teacher first gives the students an activity to do to see how well they already know the target language. This the first test. The new language is then presented to the students before they are tested again, with another activity to see if they can use the new language correctly.

The best-known way of breaking down the language into teachable parts is into items of grammar (the Structural Approach) or into functions (the Functional Approach). A recent alternative to this is the Lexical Approach, in which the language is organized into words and word patterns, multi-word units, collocations, and fixed expressions. Some coursebooks now organize their syllabus in this way. The majority of contemporary coursebooks, however, try to balance the competing demands of these and other perspectives on language.

Correcting errors in language use

We made the point at the beginning of this chapter that the four headings we are using are not simply a series of separate steps in a sequence. The teacher is constantly giving feedback to the students on their use of English. In Materials extract 6.1, for example:

1   *Test your grammar.* A student might give an answer which is comprehensible but linguistically incorrect, for example, *After this class, I'd like to going home.* This is an exercise that aims to see how much students already know about the main language point of the lesson. So, although the teacher will not want to go into detailed explanations at this stage, he or she will want to

acknowledge the successful communication, while correcting the use of the
–*ing* form of the verb. The teacher might say: *Right, so you'd like to go home.*

2 *Practice 1*. The teacher moves round the class to monitor the accuracy of
what the students are saying. The teacher might decide to correct mistakes
at the end of an exchange, or delay feedback until later (see below).

Let us look more closely at the techniques the teacher is using here. In the
introduction to Part Two, we said we would discuss appropriate techniques
for correction. Up until now however, we have been writing about giving
feedback. This was deliberate: we wanted to encourage you to give some
careful thought to the purposes of correction.

The most common meaning of correction involves pointing out to students
in one way or another how close their attempt at English is to some form
of standard English. This is important information, and giving this kind of
feedback on performance is an important part of teaching. But sometimes,
giving this type of feedback can discourage learning. It is important to use
the correction of language as an encouragement and not as punishment.
Teachers also have to think about:

- which student mistakes are signs of progress for that individual
- which mistakes a student is ready to learn from
- whether, when, and how to correct.

The main thing about correction is to give students useful information at the
right time in the right way to encourage further learning.

These distinctions are very important. If a student says *Juventus is the football team I like it best*, the important question for the teacher is not simply
whether this is standard English or not. The question is what kind of response
from the teacher will be most helpful for the student's continuing learning?
Let us look at various possible situations which lead to different answers.

1 During a *controlled exercise* or *drill* to practise relative clauses, the focus is
on *accuracy* and the teacher will want to give immediate feedback. A useful
approach is to give the student a chance for SELF-CORRECTION, if the
mistake is a slip rather than an error. The teacher might:

- pull a face to show that there was a mistake
- count out the words on his or her fingers to show where the mistake was
- echo correct by repeating the whole sentence with a questioning intonation *Juventus is the football team I like 'it' best?*
- echo correct by repeating the sentence up to the mistake and stopping:
Juventus is the football team I like . . . ?' to show where the mistake is
- use a word prompt in such as way as to highlight the mistake: *it?*
- comment directly on the mistake and talk about the language to point out
the mistake: *Here, we don't say 'I like it' in English. What's wrong with that?*

Move from self-correction, if unsuccessful, to peer correction. Ask if anyone else in the class can help. If they can, go back to the original student for a correct version. This technique is useful for:

- holding class attention
- informing the teacher about the class's general level
- encouraging the idea that students can learn from each other. The technique must be explained, however, and introduced sensitively, or it can hurt people's feelings. This is the point we noted earlier (see page 126) about eliciting answers to student questions.

The teacher gives the standard form as a last resort. If it comes to this, the teacher knows that no one in the class was capable of producing the standard form, so the first student did not really make a slip in something that had been learnt. That student made an error when attempting to say something that the class is not yet able to structure. The idea of correction is therefore not really appropriate – what is needed is more teaching.

2 If this mistake occurred during a *group activity* designed to give an opportunity for *communicative use* of the language, the focus is on *fluency*, and the teacher would not want to correct immediately. Useful ways of dealing with this are:

- collect mistakes as you walk round the class and later put them on the board for discussion without saying who made them
- write the sentence on a slip of paper and later give it to the student as something to think and perhaps ask about, and learn from
- assign to one group member the task of listening for possible mistakes and raising them as questions for discussion at the end of the task.

3 If the students are carrying out a *task* where the emphasis is on reaching the specified *outcome*, or on free, *communicative* language *use*, and not on practising language (for example, the tasks discussed in Chapter 7), the teacher may not want to correct individual errors; students' attention could be drawn to common errors, such as those caused by interference from the L1, during the focus-on-form stage of the lesson.

4 During an *informal exchange* before, during, or after the lesson, the focus is on *normal*, human *conversation* within the English-using community teacher and students share. In conversation, people very rarely focus on *the form of how* things are said, they just respond to *what* is said. What might be appropriate here would be to respond naturally and perhaps slip the correct form in without comment, with a REFORMULATION of what the student said. So, once again, in response to the statement, *Juventus is the football team I like it best*, the teacher might well say *Yes, that's a really good team. Leicester City is the team I like best.*

There is one final point to make here about mistakes and correction. We said in Chapter 2 that most learners seem to acquire the forms of a language in a very similar sequence, and this includes the sequence of non-standard forms which students produce while they are learning as part of what is called their INTERLANGUAGE (Lightbown and Spada 2006). The statement *Juventus is the football team I like it best* is certainly unlike standard English. But for the learner, making this mistake may be a necessary step in learning the standard form. Teachers need to encourage students to communicate, in the shared knowledge that this must include making mistakes if the language is to develop.

The approach outlined above aims to give appropriate feedback at the appropriate time, so as to encourage language development, while also helping students to learn from their mistakes. At its most straightforward, explicit *correction* is most appropriate during an organized practice activity, and explicit *information* about accuracy or appropriacy is most appropriate when the learner asks for it.

Summary

This chapter has presented a view of language teaching complementary to the one introduced in Chapter 7. Both approaches involve the idea that communicating in a language is an essential part of learning the language, and both are committed to the idea that knowledge about, and awareness of language play a part in language learning and language use.

Correction is a subject which arouses strong feelings in students and teachers. Consequently, it is always worth making it a topic of discussion both in class and in the staff room. In the meantime, please use at least the first question below to help you review and reflect on this and other points raised in this chapter.

Questions and activities

Think about your responses and then discuss them with a colleague if possible.

1 Look at the materials discussed in this chapter (Materials extract 6.1) and relate them to the ideas on *communication, feelings, rules, practice,* and *strategy* you read about in Chapter 2.
2 Look at the teaching suggestions in this chapter and relate the teacher's actions to the teacher roles outlined in Chapter 1.
3 At every point, the teacher could do something else. For example, in Materials extract 6.1, the dialogue in *Questions with 'like' 2*, the teacher

could carry out a choral drill with half the class taking the part of Nina and the other half the part of Sandy.

Practice 1 could be done as a class survey (or as a group survey in large classes). Some of the questions would need to be changed to be suitable for this type of activity. Each student is given one of the questions and walks around asking the other students in the class (or group) the question. He or she then reports back the answers to the rest of the class (for example, 'Five of us look like our mothers, three of us look like our fathers, two don't know').

What would you expect to gain and lose from these different methodological choices? Go through the other suggestions. What could you do differently? Why?

4 As a student, how did you feel about being corrected? As a teacher, what do you learn from recalling those feelings?

(For answers, thoughts, and comments on these questions, see page 186.)

9 IMPROVING LANGUAGE SKILLS

The communicative activities we looked at in Chapter 7 involve the use of a broad and integrated range of language skills. Although the term *four skills* is generally recognized as somewhat misleading, it remains common in ELT to refer to listening, speaking, reading, and writing in this way. These skills are also referred to as *skill areas*, each being made up of many SUBSKILLS. Although dividing language into separate skills and subskills is rather artificial, analysing it in this way gives teachers more ways of meaningfully focusing their teaching and motivating their learners.

The four skills are necessarily used in learning parts of the language. For example, when learning a new piece of grammar or a new function, students might listen to a recorded dialogue, or speak when they perform the dialogue themselves. However, in this chapter we are concerned with the opposite: with using the language to help develop the skills. In this sense, it is possible to concentrate on the teaching of skills in their own right.

Skills work is essentially based on the answers to three questions:

1 *What* do people listen to, say, read, and write? (authentic sources)
2 *Why* do people do these things? (motivation)
3 *How* do people do these things? (skills and strategies)

The answers then help us to work on how to teach these skills and strategies in English.

In ELT there are two ways of grouping skills. Firstly, listening and speaking can be grouped together, because they are the skills necessary for face-to-face communication, while reading and writing are the skills necessary for written communication.

Alternatively, listening and reading can be grouped together, because they are used for *comprehending* language, and are known as receptive skills. In contrast, speaking and writing are about *producing* language, and so are known as productive skills. As this grouping is based on similarities between the skills themselves, it is the one we shall use in this chapter.

Although we discuss the skills separately for convenience, it is likely to be more useful for learners if the teacher takes an integrated skills approach, using materials and activities involving all four skills, rather than practising them separately.

Receptive skills

Everyone in ELT agrees on the importance of providing students with meaningful language input. As students develop their receptive skills, greater quantities of input become meaningful to them, thus increasing their chances of learning the language.

Sources of authentic material

What do people *listen to* in their everyday lives? Advertisements, conversations, descriptions, directions, discussions, drama, films, instructions, interviews, lectures, news, poems, songs, speeches, sports reports, stories, talks, telephone calls, weather forecasts, podcasts, etc.

What do people *read* in their everyday lives? Apart from some of the items listed above, we could add newspapers and magazine articles, emails, letters, lists, memos, novels, reports, text messages, websites, blogs, timetables, and so on.

All of these real-life, everyday sources can be used in the language classroom as sources of authentic material. Although some of the items overlap, the language will often be very different. For example, instructions you read are expressed differently from instructions you hear.

Motivation

As a rough generalization, we can say that people listen and read for two basic reasons: for enjoyment and for information. These are the two sources of motivation the teacher has to work on. The more students use their language skills for enjoyment, the more language ability they are likely to acquire.

Listening and reading for enjoyment

What kinds of listening and reading are enjoyable to your students is something you will need to find out from them. You will then be able to give them encouragement to do this kind of listening and reading in English, without having to build in so many checks and tests that the pleasure is lost. Here are some questions and ideas which focus on encouraging out-of-class EXTENSIVE LISTENING/READING.

- Is any English language television, radio, or cinema available in your teaching situation? If so, agree on a programme or film that you will all listen to or see. Then allow some class time to discuss it.
- Is there an ongoing serial on radio or television? Go through part of a recorded episode in class and then devote a regular time to watching and discussing developments.
- Ask friends to record episodes or stories to provide a change of voice.
- If there are subtitles on DVDs or films, encourage students to experiment, sometimes looking at the subtitles, sometimes covering them up.
- Collect recordings of interesting personal events or incidents that foreigners have experienced in the country where you teach. (We would strongly advise restricting these to positive experiences!)
- Find a local source (publishers, cultural centres) of GRADED READERS or other books at the appropriate level. Would the students (or their families) be willing and able to pay for one book each if you take the trouble to organize the purchase?

It is difficult to overestimate the beneficial effect of student enjoyment of English language books, radio, and television programmes. Unfortunately however, enjoyment is not something that can be timetabled. What can be scheduled is the time teachers spend encouraging the kind of listening and reading described above. When students see that their teacher finds something important enough to spend class time on, they are also likely to take it seriously.

Listening and reading for information

In class, the focus is usually on listening and reading for information. Here, short texts of spoken or written English are used in INTENSIVE LISTENING/READING. Unfortunately, many students have learnt to listen to and read English only by working intensively on such passages. As a result, they might believe that listening and reading means starting with the first word and struggling through to the very end, with comprehension, grammar, and vocabulary being tested before the text is regarded as 'done'. This word-by-word approach may hold back their comprehension and general progress.

What the teacher needs to do is to teach subskills and strategies for listening and reading and to demonstrate that people listen and read in different ways depending on their purpose. For example, a cook will read a recipe for a new dish very carefully from beginning to end; a teacher receives the school's in-house journal and skims through it very quickly to see if there is anything of interest; a business executive going to catch a train will simply scan a timetable.

The point is not to use reading and listening to teach texts, but to use texts to teach reading and listening. So let us now take a closer look at the skills and strategies we need to teach.

Skills and strategies

The transferable skills we wish to teach will enable students to:

- skim or listen/read for gist (to get a general understanding of what a text is about)
- extract main points (when taking notes on a talk or an article)
- scan for specific information (such as a train time)
- listen/read for detail (such as instructions on how to find a house)
- listen/read for mood and infer (attitudes, feelings, moods, opinions, implications)
- evaluate (How good is this? How credible or useful is it?)
- listen/read for upshot. (What is the outcome? What have I learnt? What shall I do now?)

What teachers need to take account of is that language learners frequently find themselves understanding less than they wish they did. Therefore teachers need to encourage their students to have the confidence to carry on in spite of uncertainty and to develop a strategic approach to dealing with incoming information.

The four major strategies to encourage in students when they are listening and reading for information are to:

1 think about the purpose of listening/reading and use appropriate skills
2 think about the known information, and predict what the text and the speaker/writer will say next
3 keep thinking ahead
4 focus on what *is* understood, and use that to work out what is *not* understood, if it seems relevant or important.

It is worth pointing out to students that the skills and strategies taught in an English class are the same as those the students use in their L1, and are therefore neither new nor strange.

So far we have looked at possible sources for listening and reading materials, likely purposes for listening and reading, and skills, attitude, and strategies. Before we go on to look at the structure of a typical lesson in this area, let us consider what we know about listening and reading as the structure of a typical skills lesson comes from this:

- People understand new information in terms of what they already know, think, or feel about the subject in question.
- People usually listen and read with some purpose or interest in mind.
- Having new information should involve a change of some kind – people should know more, or think or feel differently from before, or be ready to act differently.

We will now look at the structure of a typical lesson in this area, where these various points come together in teaching.

Teaching reading skills

These considerations suggest structuring a lesson involving reading in three parts:

1 *Before the text*. The class works on the general topic in order to get students thinking about what they already know, and in order to establish a reason for reading.
2 *With the text*. The teacher uses questions and tasks to practise appropriate skills, and to make students aware of those skills.
3 *After the text*. The teacher invites the students to make a connection between the new information and their own lives.

Before the text

If you are free to choose a text, you need to balance topic, difficulty, and task in order to ensure the students are motivated, and for this, you will need to find out what interests them. It is possible to give students a difficult text so long as the task set is a simple one. Alternatively, a simple text can be used and a time limit put on the task in order to encourage an increase in reading speed. We shall return to these points when we look at individual texts.

Introduce the topic before you move on to the text. Pictures or a relevant object are very useful for this pre-reading phase. In Materials extract 9.1, a general knowledge quiz is used to introduce a reading task.

> **1** Do you know the answers to these questions?
>
>   1 What are the Earth's oldest living things?
>   2 What man-made things on Earth can be seen from space?
>   3 What is the most terrible natural disaster to have hit the Earth?
>   4 Why do women live longer than men?
>   5 Why isn't there a row 13 on aeroplanes?
>   6 Why do they drive on the left in Britain and on the right in other countries?
>   7 How many new words enter the English language every year?

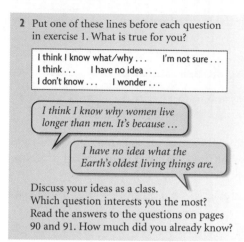

Materials extract 9.1 Soars and Soars: New Headway Plus Intermediate, page 89

The purpose of this activity is to get students thinking and talking for two reasons:

1 As they recall their previous knowledge of a topic, they are preparing themselves to understand new information.
2 In these exchanges on the topic, the teacher can elicit or present words that might be necessary in dealing with the text.

Establish a purpose for listening or reading. Outside class, people use their language skills for a purpose; in ELT the teacher needs to try to establish a purpose when asking students to use their skills. One way of doing this is to begin with questions or tasks that set the scene, and to which the students can respond from their knowledge of the topic. They can then move on to questions or tasks that demand a knowledge of the text.

Let us look at an example of the points we have made so far. Imagine a text entitled *The Florida swamps*. The teacher holds up a picture of an alligator and asks:

1 What's this?
2 Do we have these in our country?
3 Has anyone ever seen one? Where? What was it like? How did you feel when you saw it?
4 Which (other) countries do they live in?
5 What kind of climate do they live in?
6 What other animals live there?
7 In the United States, what kind of habitat do these animals live in?
8 Where exactly?
9 About how many alligators do you think there are in the United States?

Notice how the first three questions draw on the students' personal and national backgrounds, the next three move into general knowledge, and the last three turn towards the text. Some students may know answers to the last questions, some may guess, others may not. The teacher might now say:

OK, look at the text and check how many alligators there are in the USA and exactly where they live. I'll give you fifteen seconds.

As well as introducing relevant words, the introductory exchanges have given the reading some context and purpose. The time limit contributes to the development of the particular skill of scanning for specific information. Work on the text has begun.

With the text

Let us now look at Materials extract 9.2. The overall topic is still interesting facts about the world; the class has already discussed possible answers to the questions as a class in the pre-reading phase and also decided which question interests them the most.

The students are now told to read a text entitled *How well do you know your world?* and to check if their own answers to the questions were right.

Notice again how the students have been given a relatively simple task to balance the quite difficult text. This encourages them to keep on reading without worrying too much about not understanding all the words. This strategy will also help students to develop the skill of reading difficult texts for a general understanding or for specific information. As teacher, you could:

- give the students five minutes to do the task individually
- give them five minutes to check their results in pairs
- check with the whole class if there are disagreements (ask for a response; if anyone disagrees, ask for reasons before indicating whether the response is correct or not)
- point out how the key items usually come at the beginning of each paragraph in the form of a TOPIC SENTENCE, the usual place for important information. However, notice that this is not the case in Materials extract 9.2, where the writer maintains the reader's curiosity by building up to the answer, which, for most questions, is given at the end.

The next task on the text gets students to practise scanning. An appropriate procedure here would be individual work, followed by checking in pairs, and then a whole-class check.

Exercises 4 and 5 involve work on the language in the text and give students practice in reading for detail and understanding textual cohesion. (See Chapter 3.)

3 Here are the last lines of the seven answers. Which answer do they go with?

   a The country with the highest life expectancy is Japan – 84 years for women and 77 for men.
   b If they do, one will die within a year.
   c It is likely that this explosion wiped out all the dinosaurs.
   d It's interesting to note that Samuel Johnson spent 8 years writing the first English dictionary, published in 1755.
   e You can also see fires burning in the tropical rainforest.
   f It has also endured climatic catastrophes, and nuclear bomb testing – and still it lives on!
   g However, most of them are former British Colonies.

4 Here are seven questions, one for each text. What do the underlined words refer to?

   1 Where is the oldest one in the world?
   2 Why is this difficult to see from space?
   3 How many of them does it accept every year?
   4 How did they become extinct?
   5 Why don't most countries do this like the British?
   6 Do they have a thirteenth floor?
   7 Why are they more likely to have accidents?

   Answer questions 1–7.

5 These numbers are from the texts. What do they refer to?

4,600	15	200	65 million
14	six	4,000	193

Producing a class poster

6 What else would you like to know about the world? Work in groups and write some questions. Think of:

   • places (countries, cities, buildings)
   • people (customs, languages, superstitions, famous people)
   • things (machines, gadgets, transportation, etc.)
   • plants and animals

   Check round the class to see if anyone can answer your questions

7 Choose two questions you wrote in exercise 6 and research the answers. You could use the Internet or an encyclopedia.

   Make them into a poster for your classroom.

Unit 11 · Tell me about it!

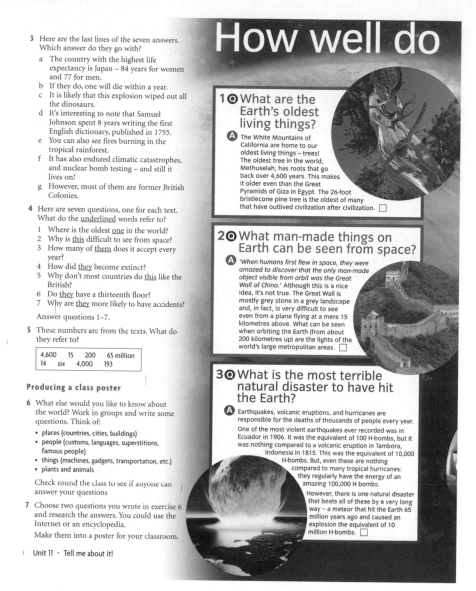

How well do

1 Q What are the Earth's oldest living things?

A The White Mountains of California are home to our oldest living things – trees! The oldest tree in the world, Methuselah, has roots that go back over 4,600 years. This makes it older even than the Great Pyramids of Giza in Egypt. The 26-foot bristlecone pine tree is the oldest of many that have outlived civilization after civilization. ☐

2 Q What man-made things on Earth can be seen from space?

A *'When humans first flew in space, they were amazed to discover that the only man-made object visible from orbit was the Great Wall of China.'* Although this is a nice idea, it's not true. The Great Wall is mostly grey stone in a grey landscape and, in fact, is very difficult to see even from a plane flying at a mere 15 kilometres above. What can be seen when orbiting the Earth (from about 200 kilometres up) are the lights of the world's large metropolitan areas. ☐

3 Q What is the most terrible natural disaster to have hit the Earth?

A Earthquakes, volcanic eruptions, and hurricanes are responsible for the deaths of thousands of people every year. One of the most violent earthquakes ever recorded was in Ecuador in 1906. It was the equivalent of 100 H-bombs, but it was nothing compared to a volcanic eruption in Tambora, Indonesia in 1815. This was the equivalent of 10,000 H-bombs. But, even these are nothing compared to many tropical hurricanes: they regularly have the energy of an amazing 100,000 H bombs.

However, there is one natural disaster that beats all of these by a very long way – a meteor that hit the Earth 65 million years ago and caused an explosion the equivalent of 10 million H-bombs. ☐

Materials extract 9.2 (Continued)

Progression from general to more detailed reading is a common way of developing reading skills. It is useful for students because it enables them to become familiar with the text initially without worrying too much about how much they understand. They are then able to focus more on the specific detail of meaning and the language used.

Another useful activity is to ask students to deduce the meaning of new words from the context, so that they do not feel they have to reach for the dictionary every time they come across a new word. In the *How well do you know your world?* text the teacher might pick out the words *outlived*,

Materials extract 9.2   Soars and Soars: New Headway Plus Intermediate,
page 90–91

landscape, earthquake, childbirth, label, banquet, right-handed for the students to guess at.

As teacher, you could:

- Do one example with the class, pointing out how the meaning of the word or phrase is actually given close to it in the text.
- Tell the students to work in pairs to define each term, or to produce another sentence in which the term is used appropriately. The point of giving them this kind of choice is to encourage involvement by different

types of learners. (When giving out a task based on a list of items, it is often worth telling different pairs to start the list at different points. Say, for example *You two start with (a), you two with (b), you two with (c) ...,* etc. This avoids getting to the feedback stage and discovering that no one has done the last two examples.)

- Ask pairs to share a response they are pleased with. Try to get a definition and an appropriate usage for each item.

It is important not to go on working with a text until everything has been squeezed out of it. Some students will be reluctant to move on from a text until they feel that they have understood every detail, but part of learning to read efficiently is learning to move away from dependence on total comprehension.

At the same time, we do not want unhappy students! One possible teaching strategy is to:

- make sure that students are aware of the skills you are teaching
- explain that your approach means you will read many more texts
- encourage those who feel a continuing need for total comprehension to use their new skills to work on the texts in their own time.

The exercises we have looked at here are good examples of how ELT sets out to teach reading, rather than endlessly test comprehension. If you find that the materials you are using consist of texts followed by comprehension questions, try to adopt some of the techniques found in ELT books and apply them to your texts. (See Chapter 10 for suggestions on using test questions for teaching.)

After the text

After-text, or post-reading activities are a good opportunity for the teacher to introduce one of the other skills. The most common is probably a speaking or writing task, usually on some aspect of the text topic. The post-reading activity in Materials extract 9.2 is an example of an integrated skills activity, where students are asked to complete a small project in groups. This involves them in *speaking* and *listening* as they plan their project and interview their classmates to find answers to their questions; in *reading* as they research their chosen topic; and in *writing* as they prepare their poster. At this point we are clearly concerned with the students' productive skills, and we shall turn to those later. (See page 150.)

Teaching listening skills

Learner difficulties with listening

This section on the receptive skills has so far focused on reading, but for many learners listening is equally important. Although the principles of teaching listening skills are very similar to those of teaching reading skills, there is one obvious difference between them. With a written text, learners can go backwards and forwards at will; the text stays there for them. A spoken text is usually only there for the moment it is spoken and that is probably why listening is the skill that learners often find the most difficult, convinced that they will not understand a word anyway. If students panic over a few unknown words, they can easily miss the whole point of a message.

Here are some of the things that concern learners about listening (adapted from Ur, 1996):

- They believe that they have to understand every word, which worries and stresses them if they miss something.
- They worry that they cannot understand fast, natural, native-sounding speech.
- They think they need to hear things more than once to understand, but in real life they do not get a second chance.
- They find it difficult to 'keep up' with all the information they are getting and feel they do not have time to think ahead and predict.
- If the listening goes on a long time, they get tired and find it more difficult to concentrate.

Before we discuss these further, you might like to think through what the teacher can do to help solve these difficulties.

Learners can be greatly helped in developing their listening skills if they are constantly reassured that they do not have to understand everything. Indeed, even in their L1 people do not listen to every word they hear. Giving learners a lot of practice in listening either for gist or for specific detail, for example, can demonstrate that understanding everything is not necessary.

Other useful ways of making listening less stressful for learners is by activating their background knowledge and developing their prediction skills. Pre-listening tasks can be used for this purpose, as well as for pre-teaching key vocabulary. In longer listenings, the teacher can also stop the recording at certain points and ask the students to predict the next section. This has the added advantage of not demanding a lengthy span of concentration.

Students' concern about needing to hear things more than once to understand can be overcome by allowing them to listen to a recording again. In real-life conversation, asking for repetition, clarification, and confirmation are a natural part of communication, an option not available in the classroom. The more competent students become in listening, the less likely they are to need to hear recordings twice.

A procedure for teaching listening

When teaching listening then, it is important to build up the students' sense of purpose and strategy, coupled with an attitude of confidence in the face of possible uncertainty. Let us look now in some detail at how listening skills are practised in Materials extract 9.3.

6 LISTENING & SPEAKING

a Read the beginning of a newspaper article and then talk to a partner:

1 Do you (or your family) ever do any of these things while driving a car?

2 Which three do you think are the most dangerous? Number them 1–3 (1 = the most dangerous).

Which of these things is the most dangerous when you're driving a car?

- making a call on your mobile
- listening to your favourite music
- listening to music you don't know
- opening a packet of crisps or a can of drink
- picking up a specific CD from the passenger seat
- talking to other passengers

A car magazine tested car drivers in a driving simulator. The drivers had to 'drive' in the simulator and at the same time do the things in the list above. The results of the tests were surprising (and worrying).

b **2.15** Now listen to a road safety expert talking about the tests. Number the activities 1–6. Were your top three right?

c Listen again and answer the questions.

1 What should you do when you are driving?

2 Why is opening a packet of crisps or a can so dangerous?

3 What do people often do when they pick up a CD?

4 What gets worse when drivers are talking on the phone?

5 How do people drive when they are listening to their favourite music?

6 What happens if the music is fast and heavy?

7 What's the main problem when drivers talk to other passengers?

8 Why is listening to music you don't know the least dangerous?

d Look at the statements below and decide whether you agree or disagree. Tick (✔) the ones you agree with and put a cross (✘) next to the ones you disagree with. Think about your reasons.

Drivers should not use any kind of phone when they are driving.

The minimum age for riding a motorbike should be 25.

People who drink and drive should lose their licence for life.

The speed limit on motorways should be 100 kilometres an hour.

Cyclists are just as dangerous as car drivers.

Speed cameras do not stop accidents.

People over 70 are more dangerous drivers than young people.

e In groups, give your opinions on each sentence. Do you agree?

Materials extract 9.3   Oxenden and Latham-Koenig: New English File Intermediate, page 31

1 *Pre-listening.* Exercises a1 and a2 constitute the pre-listening phase of these materials and have multiple purposes. They:

- create interest in the topic of the listening by personalizing it
- activate background knowledge of dangerous driving
- pre-teach useful vocabulary by listing dangerous activities which are then discussed in the listening

- give students a ranking task to do, as they have to agree on the three most dangerous activities
- take an integrated skills approach by developing reading and speaking skills in preparation for listening.

2 *While listening.* Students need to have a specific reason for listening:

- In Exercise b, the students are given a specific purpose for listening that relates back directly to the work they did in the pre-listening phase. Notice how they are given a non-linguistic task to complete and because they are asked to listen to the interview to see if their own ranking of the activities is the same, they are likely to be motivated to listen. Notice too how the initial listening activity involving listening for gist and a very general understanding is likely to be sufficient for them to complete the task successfully.
- In Exercise c, the students are asked to listen again, this time for detailed information to answer the questions, so the materials move from more general understanding to more detailed understanding. This is a common approach to developing listening skills.

3 *Post-listening.* The post-listening phase in these materials consists of an opinion-gap task and practises speaking skills. Alternative post-listening activities could be:

- writing-focused, for example, writing a letter to a newspaper about the behaviour of drivers
- project-focused, for example, preparing a radio chat show on the topic
- language-focused, for example, looking at the transcript of the interview and noticing all the expressions of comparison. Be careful when looking at transcripts to focus only on certain aspects of the language. The risk is that this becomes an exercise in understanding everything, which can undermine the message that this is not necessary.

Variety in listening

In Chapter 3 we looked at the idea of different varieties of English, or Englishes. As we noted, the majority of communication in the world in English is between people for whom it is not their first language. So, from the point of view of developing listening skills, students need to be exposed to as wide a variety of Englishes as possible. Recent coursebooks try to include a variety of accents, including those of speakers of English as a lingua franca. The Internet sites with ELT materials and video sites listed at the back of the book also have listening material with a variety of accents. (See pages 201–202.) Another way in which learners can be exposed to varieties of English is through what Harmer (2007) calls 'live listening', for which the teacher invites visitors into the classroom. This form of listening has the advantage of ensuring communication is two-way and meaningful, as students are also involved in producing the language. It is to the productive skills that we now turn.

Productive skills

There is disagreement among ELT professionals about the nature of the productive skills of speaking and writing. Some people argue that when students produce language, they are demonstrating what they have already learnt. Others argue that communicating in the language is part of the learning process itself. Teachers, at least, can be reasonably sure that an emphasis on communicative language production will give them feedback on what students have learnt, while arguably also assisting students' learning.

Authentic sources and motivation

The types of text people produce when they speak and write are, naturally, the same ones they listen to and read. (See page 138 for lists of these text types.) However the productive skills of writing and speaking require the learners to produce their own texts. Moreover, these texts need to be appropriate for a particular purpose and audience, but are produced in a language classroom, usually without any such audience.

As with the receptive skills, the teacher's task is to involve students in the types of language use which motivate them, while teaching them skills and strategies they will be able to use independently.

Skills and strategies

The most important language production skills are an ability to:

- develop meanings logically and clearly
- express unambiguously the function of the message
- use language appropriate to the people being addressed.

A necessary strategy for language learners to develop is the ability to communicate ideas which they do not know exactly how to express in the L2. (See Chapter 3, pages 36–37, for some suggestions in this area.)

Guidance and autonomy in speaking and writing

In the process of creating original and personal texts, there needs to be a balance between teacher guidance and autonomy, as students move towards greater independence. There are essentially three ways of combining these features. Students are asked to:

1 work with a model and personalize it
2 discuss and plan what they want to say or write
3 DRAFT, receive comment, and RE-DRAFT their text.

Work with a model and personalize it

This approach also underlies the teaching sequence in Chapter 8. Materials extract 9.4 is an example of guided writing. Notice how students analyse the language of the model (parts A and B) and then focus on its organization (part C) before being asked to personalize it to produce their own message.

Writing A message of apology

A Read for the main idea

1 Which is the worst mistake? Decide with a partner. Compare with the class.
    1 I forgot to reply to your last email.
    2 I forgot to send you a message on your birthday.
    3 I sent you a virus by mistake.
    4 I thought your email was junk mail and I deleted it.
    5 I wrote an email to someone else and I sent it to you by mistake.

2 Read this email. How well does Paul know Jen?

> Hi ,Jen, I'm sorry but I think I've sent you a virus by mistake. because I opened an email this morning, and I didn't know who sent it but the subject was just 'Good News!', and It had an attachment called 'Message from a Friend' and I opened it without thinking and It was a virus and I think it went into my address book and sent an email to all my contacts so if you got an email from me, DON'T open the attachment because If the virus gets into your computer, it will go to all the people in your address book and I'm really sorry about this, all the best from Paul. : (

3 When we apologize, we often give details to explain what happened. What details does Paul give?

4 Work with a partner. How would you apologize for the other mistakes in exercise 1?

B Check the style

5 **8E.1▶** Read the email again and listen. Answer the questions.
    1 Is it easy to understand? Why?/Why not?
    2 How many sentences are there?
    3 How could you make it better?

6 Use these symbols to edit the email, and change the punctuation if you want.
    //   new line
    /   new sentence
    ~~and~~ delete word

    Example Hi Jen,// I'm sorry but I think I've sent you a
              virus by mistake./ ~~because~~ I opened an ...

7 **8E.2▶** Listen. Does the speaker pause in the same places where you put // and /? Now check the audio script on ≫ p.156.

C Organizing an apology message

8 Put this email in order.
    a ☐ All the best, Jen
    b ☐ Could you send it again?
    c ☐ Hi Paul
    d ☐ It came together with a lot of junk emails and I deleted them all.
    e ☐ Sorry, I've deleted the email you just sent by mistake.
    f ☐ Sorry about that!
    g ☐ Then I remembered there was a message from you, but it was too late.

9 Match parts of the message with the sentences in exercise 8.
    1 Greeting = ☐ c
    2 Why I am sorry. = ☐
    3 What happened. = ☐ and ☐
    4 What to do (or not to do) next. = ☐
    5 Final apology. = ☐
    6 Goodbye. = ☐

10 Work with a partner. Find the same parts of the message in Paul's email in exercise 2.

ABC Put it all together

11 Think of a situation where you did something bad to someone by mistake. Answer the questions.
    1 What did you do?
    2 Why did you do it?
    3 What did the other person do/say?

12 Write an email message to apologize. Remember to include the parts of the message in exercise 9.

13 Check your partner's message.
    Are the sentences too long?
    Do they give details to explain what happened?

Materials extract 9.4 Hancock and McDonald: English Result
Pre-intermediate, page 84

In this example, the teacher and the materials exercise a degree of control in order to give the learners a structure within which they express themselves, using their own information and imagination.

A model can also be a useful approach for teaching speaking strategies. The exercise in Materials extract 9.5 draws students' attention to appropriacy in spoken language use, and also teaches them short answer forms together with follow-up comments as a useful conversation strategy.

---

1 **T 1.5** Listen to the breakfast conversation. How does Emma feel?

Dad	Good morning! Did you have a nice time yesterday?
Emma	Yes.
Dad	Do you want breakfast?
Emma	No.
Dad	Have you had any coffee?
Emma	Yes.
Dad	Is Nadia coming round tonight?
Emma	No.
Dad	OK. Are you leaving for school soon?
Emma	Yes. Bye!

2 **T 1.6** Listen to a similar conversation. What are the differences?

3 Complete the conversation.

Dad	Good morning! Did you have a nice time yesterday?
Emma	Yes, _____. I went round to Nadia's house.
Dad	Do you want breakfast?
Emma	No, _____, thanks. I'm not hungry.
Dad	Have you had any coffee?
Emma	Yes, _____. I don't want any more, thanks.
Dad	Is Nadia coming round tonight?
Emma	No, _____. She's going out for dinner with her family.
Dad	OK. Are you leaving for school soon?
Emma	Yes, _____. I'm going right now. Bye!

T 1.6 Listen again and check.

4 Close your books. Try to remember the conversation.

Materials extract 9.5 Soars and Soars: New Headway Plus Intermediate,
page 8

After being presented with this model of conversational diversity and appropriacy, students are asked to conduct a class survey, where they ask and answer questions such as 'Have you seen any good films lately?'. Their contribution is the addition of some extra information to their replies.

In Chapter 3 we mentioned discourse, text types, and text structure. Sample texts are important here. Students are unlikely to be able to write an appropriate book review, for example, unless they have actually seen a book review in English. However, to produce longer texts in a certain genre, copying a model from a book or from the board is not enough. Students need to be aware of how a certain type of text is organized and to think about the language used to achieve this organization. Look back at Chapter 3, Materials extract 3.5 for an example of how this works. (See page 46.)

Discuss and plan

We now focus on extended speaking because in language classrooms learners are rarely given opportunities to speak at any length. And yet this is something people do all the time outside the classroom when they tell stories, describe things, tell jokes, and so on.

One particularly way of practising extended speech is to follow up a group discussion with an activity where all the groups report back to the class. This would include the report stage of task-based teaching that we looked at in Chapter 7.

It is important to set up this report-back stage following group discussions for several reasons:

- the expectation of it focuses group members on their task
- preparation of it encourages the group to reflect on what they have done
- it ensures that, even if some of the language used in discussion is not English, the work has to be talked about in English
- students have to plan what they are going to say, which gives them the opportunity to discuss how best to do this and to ask for guidance and correction
- students take turns to make an extended statement in English.

Let us go back to Materials extract 6.2 This activity has two report-back stages: first individuals or pairs join together in a group and present their arguments. Having discussed the arguments and decided on the two best ones, the group then presents these to the whole class. When a group has finished, or towards the end of the allotted time, one or more of its members can be asked to prepare to make a report. The teacher may provide a framework in order to help the report develop clearly. You might say:

Remember to tell us which measures you are in favour of and why.

The variety of extended speaking genres used here can be increased by asking each group to make a formal presentation with visual aids, rather than reporting back informally.

By asking students to work first in pairs and then in groups, to come to their own decisions, and to report back on the outcome, learners are given an opportunity to clarify their ideas and the time to plan what to say, all of which helps their language development (Foster 1996). The suggestion is also that students learn from each other; the teacher guides them and encourages cooperation and independence.

The student(s) making the report will be under some pressure while 'performing' in front of teacher and class, so the teacher needs to ignore linguistic errors as long as the message is clear. If the message is not clear, the teacher rephrases what the student has said and checks it with the student, for example:

Excuse me a moment, Felipe. Are you saying that you are in favour of expanding current business activity?

Draft, comment, and re-draft

Let us now look at this approach in terms of extended writing. Writing is a more deliberate act than speaking, and it leaves a permanent record, so writers need to be careful about how the record looks. On the other hand, teachers want learners to make genuine attempts to express themselves in writing, even though this will inevitably lead to errors. One approach is to introduce PROCESS WRITING with first and second drafts at an early stage. Here is one possible teaching procedure using a process-writing approach:

- use small group or class discussion to brainstorm ideas for the writing
- feedback ideas to the whole class
- elicit suggestions for an overall organizational framework for the piece of writing
- ask students to write their first drafts
- get students to exchange their first drafts with a partner for PEER FEEDBACK
- ask students to work in pairs on revision of first drafts, including editing and proof-reading
- tell students to write individual second drafts to submit to the teacher for correction and comments or for grading if necessary.

Let us look at how this procedure might be applied with Materials extract 9.6.

1 As this writing activity follows a reading text about historical sites, the teacher may prefer to do the first two steps above together so that students can brainstorm as a class their ideas on the role of historical sites, using what they have read, while the teacher notes the points on the board.

Writing an evaluation essay

4 Read the essay title.

The role of historic sites.

Write the introduction to the essay. Remember to include a thesis statement explaining the purpose of your essay, and giving your opinion.

5 Look at the notes for the next two paragraphs for the essay. Cross out one piece of irrelevant information from each list.

1 Education
1.1 show clearly how people used to live/work
1.2 easier for children to learn and understand than books, etc. + example
1.3 can learn from earlier technologies
1.4 fun day out for the family

2 Tourism
2.1 many visitors want to visit historic sites + example
2.2 visitors bring money into local + national economy
2.3 visitors take many photographs to show their friends
2.4 visitors understand more about our culture and history

6 Write the two paragraphs, using the notes in exercise 5. Give examples. Use words and phrases from *Language for Writing* on page 47.

7 Write a conclusion to the essay. Summarize the main points and give your opinion.

8 Check your essay for purpose, content, and organization (see Study Skill p48).

STUDY SKILL
Checking your writing (4)

After completing the first draft of your essay, put it aside for a while. It is easier to check the content with 'fresh' eyes. Check for:

Purpose
Is the purpose of the essay to *describe, explain, persuade, analyse, discuss, compare,* or *evaluate*?

Content
Does the essay:
- introduce the topic clearly?
- include all the main points?
- exclude irrelevant or inappropriate information?
- give examples and explanations?
- conclude appropriately?

Organization
- Are the ideas in a logical order?
- Is the writing divided into paragraphs?
- Are ideas linked appropriately?

Materials extract 9.6 Philpot and Curnick: New Headway Academic Skills Level 3, pages 48–49

2 The teacher elicits a possible structure for an evaluation essay and writes the sections on the board.

3 Students are asked to do Exercises 4–7 individually. The teacher can monitor and check that the students have correctly identified the irrelevant information.

4 The teacher goes over the Skills Box with the students, checking that they have understood everything.

5 The students exchange essays with their partner, who uses the Skills Box to give peer feedback.

6 Students write their second draft on the basis of the PEER FEEDBACK and hand it to the teacher for correction.

You may also prefer the students to take their second drafts home, leave them for a few days and then go through the Skills Check Box themselves for self-correction, before writing a third draft.

In process writing, the students are encouraged to express themselves, and their writing is taken seriously – the emphasis has shifted to include the process of improving what they write. This process is a key element in independent language use. The teacher gets feedback on the students' language needs, and the students have a (relatively) standard piece of English as a record.

Our comments on correction in Chapter 8 (see pages 132–135) are particularly relevant here. Students must realize that you are deliberately drawing their attention to points you think they need to note in their final draft. You will not necessarily be turning everything they write into standard English. Your comments on their drafts should include reactions to what the students have to say, not only to how they have said it.

Students will produce a smaller number of texts than they might be used to, because each one will go through at least two drafts. The idea is to teach generalizable skills and this makes demands on the writing tasks themselves – that they should be meaningful and interesting enough for the students to want to express themselves well.

We have illustrated the discuss-and-plan approach to skills by talking about extended speaking and we have illustrated the draft, comment, re-draft approach in relation to writing. It is also possible to teach writing through discuss-and-plan, and speaking through draft, comment, and re-draft. If we go back to Materials extract 6.2, rather than have a report-back phase to the class, students could be asked to write a case study report to put forward their proposals.

Likewise draft, comment, re-draft would be the approach to follow if students are preparing an oral presentation, or a speech, for example.

As we have constantly reiterated in this book, it is not the case of there being *the* way of teaching. There are many ways and it is up to you to draw on your experience, to formulate what you know, and to use that knowledge to help you to construct the right way for your aims, your learners, and the context you are in.

Integrated skills

In this chapter we have mainly treated each of the four skills as separate, but this is rarely the case inside or outside the classroom. It should be clear from what we have said about the sample materials presented that coursebooks rarely present skills in isolation. The main focus in Materials extracts 9.1 and 9.2 is on reading, but students are asked to speak and listen to each other before they read the text. They can also be asked to speak to each other and compare their answers to Exercises 3, 4, and 5 in Materials extract 9.2. In Materials extract 9.6, the main focus is on writing, but students also discuss the topic and read each other's writing. And of course they have to read the exercises to answer the questions and to write the answers. So while the *focus* may be on developing a particular skill, the *activities* almost always involve all four skills.

However, it is also possible to develop more than one skill at a time deliberately, an approach that certainly reflects the ways the skills are used outside the classroom. So students might read a text and write a summary of the main points. Or they might listen to a recording, take notes and then orally summarize the main points.

All four skills can also be integrated. In theory, they can be combined in any way but, as we pointed out in Chapter 7, the most common ways in ELT involve information gathering, followed by an exchange of information or a discussion, then by some kind of information production. If we express that in terms of receptive and productive skills, the pattern is usually:

Listen/Read   →   Converse/Discuss   →   Speak/Write

Let us look at how this might work in practice by returning to Materials extract 9.3. Rather than use the pre-listening material in the book, you could bring in an article from a newspaper or magazine on the topic of dangerous driving. The class work on this text, following the principles outlined above. These activities prepare students for the listening activity, but also develop their reading skills. Listening and speaking skills can be developed by following the activities in the book. Following on from the theme of dangerous driving, a speaking activity could also be devised as:

- a formal debate, with a motion such as 'This house believes that the speed limit on motorways should be reduced to 90 kilometres an hour'. One or two students can speak for and against the motion and the class then take a vote at the end.

- a role play on dangerous driving, to include drinking and speeding, in which a worker has been injured by a drink-driver. Other characters might include a police officer, two witnesses – an old man and a young woman who has just passed her test, both of whom give their version of events.

Finally, the students can be asked to write a letter to a newspaper giving their point of view on one of the statements in Exercise d, or write an essay on the topic of road safety.

Another point emerges from the diagram above on integrating skills. The different skills are not only integrated in terms of an overall sequence of information gathering, exchange, and production. When it comes to the information exchange stage, they are integrated to the extent that they change their nature: a conversation is more than a sequence of speaking and listening turns, and it is worth giving some attention to this in its own right.

Conversations and discussions

There are times when you bring the whole class together to introduce a topic, or to listen to verbal reports, but conversations and discussions take place most effectively in small groups, where students feel less nervous about speaking and making mistakes.

If your main concern is to stimulate discussion, a fictionalized topic with a problem often works better than an abstract one. For example, the age at which young people are allowed to marry might be an interesting subject for a group of teenage students, but they might find it difficult to relate to the topic if it is presented as an abstract issue. If you introduce this topic by telling a story involving two young people who want to marry but their parents are against the match, and then ask groups to give advice and voice opinions, this is more likely to lead to involvement and result in animated discussion.

It is often the case that students have something to say, but cannot break into the discussion at the right time. You can teach them useful phrases such as, *Sorry to interrupt you*, or *I agree with (name) because* …, or *But you just said* …. You can also ask students to write such expressions on small cards. During their discussion, students have to 'play' each card by using the phrase on it in an appropriate manner.

A useful extension of this is to make and give students a different set of cards for them to choose ones they would like to try out. If you include phrases such as *Let's hear what (name) has to say about this* and *What do you think, (name)?* this teaches students who talk a lot the useful skill of drawing other people into a discussion.

Informal conversation and COLLOQUIAL language use is more difficult to practise in a language classroom because it is, by its very nature, spontaneous. We mentioned in Chapter 6 the importance of encouraging everyday exchanges in order to build a classroom community. Such exchanges can help students to develop their conversation skills. Role plays can also be useful: for example, students role play being at a party. Each student is given a card with personal information about their job, family and so on, and information about one other person at the party. They then have to mingle and chat to people until they find the person on their card. The advantage of role play is that students get the chance to practise opening and closing a conversation, something that in the classroom is normally done only by the teacher!

Summary

In developing the four skills, we constantly refer to the importance of using language from relevant sources, and producing language towards relevant ends. Skills are developed extensively (and often enjoyably) through communicative activities, as well as intensively through accurate study. A lesson on receptive skills will feature work before and after the actual text used. A lesson on productive skills will emphasize the processes of production as well as the product itself. But a lesson based on integrated skills will do all these things together in a meaningful and more natural way.

Questions and activities

Think about your responses and then discuss them with a colleague if possible.

1 Think about students with a specific purpose for learning English. Can you make a list of which types of texts and which subskills will be most important for them? Check your ideas with such a student if possible.
2 Go through the list of ideas for encouraging extensive listening and reading. Choose one. Work out a plan for how you are going to make this happen.
3 Choose a reading text and think of some questions which would lead from students' personal experience and knowledge back to the text itself.
4 The *After* text activity in Materials extract 9.2 involves a small project. How might the activities be organized and taught?
5 Plan a lesson around the listening materials in 9.3.
6 How does this chapter's comments on guidance, autonomy, and independence relate to what Chapter 8 said about careful practice and communication?
7 How many useful conversational expressions can you think of for putting on cards? Can you group them or sequence them in any way for teaching? How would you introduce them?

(For answers, thoughts, and comments on these questions, see page 187.)

10 TESTING

The majority of teachers are less likely to be asked to construct tests than to use tests and to teach in a situation where test or formal examination results are very important. In this chapter, therefore, we shall look at:

- types of test and how to use them
- the relationship between teaching and testing.

Types of test and how to use them

Purposes

The overall purpose of testing is to provide information about ability and about the learning and teaching process. Proficiency testing assesses a student's level of ability, and its main uses are as follows:

- placement tests, to put new students into the right class
- diagnostic tests, to identify students' areas of strength and weakness
- qualifications, when students take a formal examination separate from a course.

Achievement testing establishes whether a student has learnt what he or she is supposed to have learnt as a result of the teaching. This can be done by testing at the end of the course, or according to a scheme of CONTINUOUS ASSESSMENT as the course progresses. Continuous assessment may be in the form of progress tests to see how students are getting on in a course, or in the form of coursework, which is not done under test conditions.

Principles

Probably the most important principle testing shares with teaching is that there is no single 'best way' of testing. As with teaching, we have to consider our students, their backgrounds, and the purpose of the test before we can decide what is appropriate. We also have to take into account certain principles that can help us make decisions in the various contexts in which we work.

Validity and reliability

A test is valid to the extent that it actually tests what it is supposed to test. So a valid test of student ability to understand spoken English must test that and only that. If students are asked to write long answers to OPEN COMPREHEN-SION QUESTIONS and are deducted marks for poor grammar, this reduces the validity of the test as far as listening comprehension is concerned. For example, if students are asked to listen to a short account of John's holiday disaster and then asked *What happened to John?* the test will be less valid as a listening test if the grammatical accuracy of the students' answers is taken into account as part of their marks.

A test is reliable to the extent that it produces the same result under the same circumstances. So, if two people of the same ability do the test, or if the same person does it twice, they should score the same.

Subjectivity and standardization

Validity and reliability usually pull in different directions. Communication is subjective, and tests of communicative ability should include a subjective element if they are to be valid. If two students are tested to discover if they would be able to communicate socially on a trip to an English-speaking country, the teacher or examiner might decide simply to have a half-hour conversation with them. Such a conversational exchange would be valid, and the examiner would trust his or her subjective opinion.

But subjective judgements cannot be repeated consistently; some tests have to be carried out on a large scale and involve many individual markers. If there are fifty students in the above situation and the examiners had to choose which five would be best able to make the trip, there would need to be some way of standardizing responses in order to maintain reliability. Although language testing cannot be objective in a real sense, techniques to help standardize marking do exist, and the expression OBJECTIVE TESTING is used to describe the process. (See *Recognition* below.)

In view of these considerations, test design needs to balance validity and reliability, subjectivity and standardization. The result is that no test is or can be perfectly valid or perfectly reliable.

Procedures

It is possible to test students' ability in English by setting a task and seeing whether or not they can carry it out. One such task might be: *Students must*

*give accurate directions from Point A to Point B on a street map to someone who
cannot see the map.*

So, if you look back at Materials extract 4.1 (see page 58), you might ask a
student *'We're in the Tourist Information Office. Can you tell me how to get to
the museum?'* If the student's directions get you to the museum, the student
meets the criterion and passes. This is called *criterion-referenced* testing. It
gives yes/no information about students' specific abilities in English. It does
not give detailed linguistic information, nor does it allow students in a class
to be ranked.

In *norm-referenced* testing students are assessed by comparison with other
students in the group. This makes it possible to rank students according
to their level of achievement with respect to their peers. Norm-referenced
testing focuses on the language itself in one of two ways:

1 *Recognition.* Students are given language options and asked to choose the
   correct one.
2 *Production.* Students have to make up their own language responses.

Recognition

Recognition items require a choice from the students. If there are several
options to choose from, these are called multiple-choice questions. Multiple-
choice tests are often used for testing discrete grammar points, for example:

Please take _____ one of these.

A: a   B: any   C: the   D: an

One of the attractions of testing by recognition is that marking is quick, easy
and, in itself, objective. This means that tests are relatively reliable (in the tech-
nical sense we used above). On the other hand, many people question their
validity in terms of exactly what is being tested. Good multiple-choice questions are notoriously difficult to write: you need to be certain, for example,
that there is not more than one possible correct answer, even in different
contexts. You also need to make sure that the correct item does not stand out
in some way, perhaps by being a lot longer or shorter than the distractors (the
wrong answers). It is important to try out your own multiple-choice items
on competent users of English before trying them out on students. You may
be surprised at the results!

Production

When students are asked to produce language in a test, the result is often an
increase in validity and a loss in reliability. Having said that, the degree of
reliability will vary according to what we ask the students to produce. For
example, a test based on sentence transformation, such as:

Rewrite the following sentence with the passive:

They have increased the price of petrol again.

is likely to be reasonably reliable (although we could question the validity of what it is actually testing). A test based on sentence completion, such as:

If I were offered a job in the United States, I …

may be less reliable. In other words, the freer the students are in their language production for the test, the less reliable the test is.

Answers involving free production can never be totally reliable and the test will always be a relatively SUBJECTIVE TEST. This is a perennial difficulty in testing language production. However, there are three ways of making the test as reliable as possible:

1 *Double marking*

Given that real objectivity is impossible in testing communication, the best hope is to get at least two subjective opinions. Where they disagree strongly, a third may be necessary. If you are involved in a team which has to test a large number of students in spoken or written English, you should all assess a small number of them together first.

2 *Analysis*

If a piece of writing or speech is broken down into different areas of assessment, this could help to make similar assessments of the whole. For the above interview, for example, there could be separate headings for pronunciation, grammar, fluency, and appropriacy. Such headings should of course be agreed between colleagues.

3 *Ranking*

If a scale of ability can be agreed in advance, this can also be used as the basis for standardizing marking. The next step beyond the kind of yes/no criterion we looked at above is to establish three grades: unsatisfactory, satisfactory, more than satisfactory. Most teachers can reach agreement on the basis of these three grades, but circumstances may force you to subdivide each one further. With each further division, there is likely to be less agreement. To counter this, it can be helpful to agree a description of what you mean by each grade. In terms of pronunciation, for example, you might agree the following typical definitions:

- More than satisfactory: The listener has no difficulty in understanding what the student said; clear sounds, appropriate stress and intonation.
- Satisfactory: The student is comprehensible, but demands effort from the listener; sounds are sometimes unclear, some sounds pronounced inaccurately, stress and intonation not always helpful

- Unsatisfactory. The listener frequently could not understand what the student said; intonation did not clarify or enliven; monotonous or staccato delivery.

International language tests (see below) use bands and descriptors at each level to grade test-takers and you might be able to adapt their scales for your own tests. For example, the Cambridge ESOL First Certificate English (FCE) examination has five bands for the assessment of writing. Band 5 is described as follows:

> "… the candidate's writing fully achieves the desired effect on the target reader. All the content points required in the task are included and expanded appropriately. Ideas are organized effectively, with the use of a variety of linking devices and a wide range of structure and vocabulary. The language is well developed, and any errors that do occur are minimal and perhaps due to ambitious attempts at more complex language. Register and format which is consistently appropriate to the purpose of the task and the audience is used."

The combined effects of multiple marking, analysis of tested items, and agreement on scales of ability can partly make up for the lack of reliability inherent in language production tests.

Cloze tests

Finally in this section, let us look at one type of test which enables us to draw together several of the points made so far, which can be very useful to teachers who:

- need an idea of the general language ability of a group of students
- regularly teach the same level of student
- are involved in placement testing.

The procedure is as follows:

1 Find a 400–500 word text you would expect your students to be able to read and understand.
2 Leave the first few sentences intact and then delete every seventh word.
3 Tell students to write in the missing words.
4 Mark each word correct if it is the word originally used by the writer.

Here is an example of a possible cloze test (with answers written in), using Materials extract 9.2:

> Why do women live longer than men?

> Women generally live about six years longer than men. Evidence suggests that boys are the weaker sex at birth, which means that more die in infancy. Men also have a greater risk _of_ heart disease than women, and they _have_ heart attacks earlier in life. Men _smoke_ more than women, and their behaviour _is_ generally more aggressive, particularly when driving, _so_ they are more likely to die _in_

accidents. Also, men are more often __in__ dangerous occupations, such as construction work.

__Historically__ , women died in childbirth and __men__ in wars. So unmarried women and __philosophers__ often lived to great ages. __Now__ childbearing is less risky and there __are__ fewer wars.

By deleting every seventh word and only accepting the word originally used by the writer, greater reliability is ensured as there is no discretion involved.

You are looking for a text on which the average class score is between 53 per cent and 60 per cent. This indicates that your students should be just about able to read and understand the original text on their own. If you build up a small collection of such texts, you can use them to:

- compare average standards across different groups, and possibly adjust your teaching appropriately
- check whether new students should join your class, or if they are likely to find the work too easy or too difficult
- help with the future placement of students at the beginning of the next teaching session
- develop your own appreciation of your students' language abilities as you get better at selecting appropriate texts.

Cloze tests are easy-to-produce proficiency tests that are acceptably valid, reasonably reliable, and quick to mark. They are also on the borderline between production tests and recognition tests, in that they call upon the students to produce the missing word, but so much context is given that one could say that students are called upon to recognize which word is missing. You can go through them and draw out information about discrete points of language use, although their main function is as an integrated test of ability.

Peer and self-assessment

So far we have looked at what we might term 'traditional' testing, in which the teacher assesses the students in some way. But especially (although not only) in communication-to-language approaches to ELT, the teacher might want to look at alternative ways of assessing students, such as PEER ASSESSMENT or SELF-ASSESSMENT. These forms of assessment are more STUDENT-CENTRED, allowing learners to learn from the assessment process itself.

Peer assessment

Students can learn a lot both by evaluating the work of their peers and by having their own work evaluated in this way. However, they are unlikely to get very far if they are simply told to assess a piece of work. For peer assessment to be successful, students must be clear as to what the criteria for assessment are. One way of doing this would be to give students an evaluation checklist. For example, if pairs of students are evaluating the ability of another pair to express their opinions in a debate, the following checklist would be appropriate:

Tick the box every time you hear one of the following functions used appropriately and write down some examples of the expressions used.

Expressing an opinion
Examples
Agreeing
Examples
Disagreeing
Examples
Interrupting politely
Examples

Figure 10.1 Peer assessment evaluation checklist

Another way would be to allow the students themselves to decide what to assess and to work as a group to draw up the ASSESSMENT CRITERIA. At first, students will need a lot of help and guidance from the teacher, but as they become more used to this form of evaluation, they will be able to draw up and apply their own assessment criteria. There are many different ways of organizing peer assessment; some possibilities are:

- Individual work is assessed by another individual; pairs assess each other's work or students are put in groups and each member of the group assesses the work of every other member. This way of organizing peer assessment could be used in a process approach to writing. (See Chapter 9.)
- Group work is assessed by another student from outside the group. This can be used to evaluate speaking by having a student act as 'monitor' during group discussion and evaluate the contributions to the discussion. Evaluation can be both of individual contributions and the group as a whole.
- Group work or individual work is assessed by the whole class; this can be done in the case of group or individual presentations, for example, where the rest of the class acts as the audience and then evaluates the presentation.
- Group work is assessed by each member of the group; this could be a way of evaluating projects, for example. Students can evaluate the way the group worked on the project, the final product, and/or their own contribution to it.

If such ideas are new in the teaching context, then just as with peer correction, learners may not see peer assessment as appropriate. They may feel embarrassed to be asked to evaluate, or feel they lose face by being evaluated in this way by their classmates. If this is the case, the teacher has to exercise great caution and to be sure the learners understand and agree with the potential value of peer assessment.

Self-assessment

Much of what we have said about peer assessment also applies to self-assessment. Self-assessment enables students to reflect on their learning strategies and their progress. As we said in Chapter 2, such increased awareness is an important part of learner autonomy. As with peer assessment, students cannot learn to assess their own progress without initial guidance. One way is for the teacher and students to agree a set of goals. Achievement can then be self-assessed against the achievement of these goals. If you are concerned that students will just give themselves high marks, experience shows that students are tougher on themselves and their peers than the teacher is!

It is probably fair to say that both self- and peer assessment are more suitable to formative assessment rather than a summative test as defined below.

Portfolios

A useful tool in assessment is the individual portfolio. This is a collection of the student's work and can be used to document his or her progress, both in terms of the learning process and in terms of achievement. Students and teachers can decide together what the portfolio should contain. This might include pieces of work such as written assignments, results and/or copies of any class tests or informal assessments, certificates from international examination bodies, samples of project work, oral presentations, and so on. Portfolios can be used for:

- Formative assessment. This provides feedback on progress during the course, from which the student can learn. This can also be seen as a form of continuous assessment.
- Summative assessment. This is formal assessment with final grades and is usually done with end-of-course tests. However, it can also be done through continuous assessment if students have specific milestones to achieve as they go along.

Portfolios have been popular for some time. The Council of Europe, for example, has developed a European Language Portfolio (ELP) to support plurilingualism and pluriculturalism. The ELP consists of three parts:

- *Language passport.* This is a record of formal qualifications and self-assessment based on the Common European Framework of Reference for Languages (CEFR), a series of descriptors of ability that can be applied to any language and used to assess achievement in language learning.
- *Language biography.* This is a record of personal language-learning history. The purpose is to help students to evaluate learning objectives, and to reflect on language learning and inter-cultural experiences.

- *Dossier*. This is a collection of work chosen by the students to illustrate language skills and achievements.

We have looked at some important principles and procedures in language testing. We shall now move on to the relationship between teaching and testing.

Teaching and testing

While it is convenient to have a separate chapter on language testing, it is also important to think of testing as a part of the teaching and learning process. Many teachers will tell you that testing is the worst part of the job, but that simply confirms that it *is* part of the job.

Two real problems with testing are that it often involves:

1 adapting what you do to powers beyond your control and
2 coming to terms with failure.

Adapting to powers beyond your control

Tests frequently have a negative impact on teaching, when language *teaching* is replaced by constant language *testing* in order to prepare students for formal examinations. This phenomenon is known as the *backwash effect*. With class achievement testing, however, it is often possible to shape the tests to the teaching or to develop the teaching and testing together in the most appropriate way for the students.

The last few years has seen a growing trend towards requiring students to take formal, internationally recognized examinations in English. The requirement may be for entry to an English-medium university, or to get a new job or promotion. This step towards international standardization of qualifications has its advantages, but the disadvantages are that such tests are very expensive, and the concurrent increase in centralizing power for the dominant institutions in the field should not be ignored.

The main tests recognized around the world are those offered by Cambridge ESOL (English to Speakers of Other Languages), together with TOEFL (Test of English as a Foreign Language) and IELTS (International English Language Testing Service). Unless you teach only within your country's state education system, you can be fairly certain that at some stage in your career you will be preparing students for one or more of these examinations.

When you teach an examination course, you take on an extra responsibility. The students in your class have a right to expect you to help them to pass that examination. There are two extreme positions here, both of which are honourable. The first one expresses a sense of responsibility to the principles of good teaching, and says:

I teach them English the best way I can, and with that English they ought to be able to pass any examination.

The second expresses a sense of responsibility to the students and says:

The students are here to pass the examination, so that is what I teach them. They can worry about 'communicative ability' when they need it.

The first position runs the risk of sacrificing the students to educational principles. The second runs the risk of teaching to an examination and perhaps destroying any further interest the students may have in the language.

The second of these positions is the more common because it involves personal loyalty to students and because teachers see students' examination failure as personally threatening. This is why, if teaching and testing are in conflict, testing usually wins out. Let us look at some ways in which we might find a useful way forward.

- *Talk to the students about the situation.* The teacher may know what is going on in class and how it relates to an examination, but the students may not. That applies to every new class.
- *Be positive.* As with materials, teachers might want to change an unsatisfactory examination, but they should not pass on negativity about it to the students.
- *Get to know the examination.* Both teachers and students should be familiar with old examination papers, and these may also come with a written statement of what the examination sets out to test. If the examination in question is an international one, there will almost certainly be published books available on test preparation, examination techniques, common mistakes, and some will include practice tests.
- *Distinguish between language skills and examination techniques.* If the students are preparing for an examination made up mostly of multiple-choice grammar items, some might worry about spending time on communicative activities. You can point out that in this instance the activity is for language learning, and that you will cover the necessary examination techniques in your language focus after the activity.
- *Use examination techniques as the basis of communicative activities.* Any recognition item that requires a choice can be the basis for discussion in pairs, groups, or all together; just as any test item that requires language production can be the basis for cooperative preparation, redrafting, and assessment, also in pairs, groups, or all together.

Furthermore, by relating discussion, cooperation, and assessment to examination techniques, you can help to reduce examinations anxiety. Here is one technique for working on multiple-choice grammar tests in this situation:

1 Collect common mistakes as you listen to a group activity. For example, *I live here since January*.
2 Write each sentence on the board or OHP, or prepare a worksheet with a blank where the mistake was:

I ___ here since January. (to live)

3 Elicit suggestions for filling the blank and write them all on the board.
4 Ask the students to talk about and choose one or more possible answers.

This technique is useful for raising grammatical awareness and demystifying multiple-choice questions. It can also make students more aware of the importance of context as they see different possibilities fit.

Coming to terms with failure

In spite of all a teacher's best efforts, it is inevitable that some students will fail. Student failure can be just as difficult for teachers as it is for students. To work with people throughout a course, to get to know them, come to like them, and then to tell them that they have failed an examination, particularly one you yourself set and marked, is an experience non-teachers do not know about. It may be helpful to bear in mind that we *teach people* and we *evaluate language ability*. We do not evaluate people.

In this context, the importance of progress tests cannot be overemphasized. If you are teaching a course with an examination at the end of it, make sure that you discover early on which students are lagging behind and tell them immediately. Try to balance warning with encouragement, without building false hopes. Both warning and the encouragement are signs of your professional seriousness and both depend on your ability to assess. If it is too early to use items like the ones in the examination, a cloze test will give you a general indication of ability.

Another aspect of poor examination results is that widespread student failure would indicate a need to review your course, your teaching, and your tests, and would require guidance and further training.

Summary

'Testing', like 'correction', is for many people a word with negative overtones. The two challenges teachers face are, first, to make testing an acceptable way of gathering useful information to help learners and teachers and, second, not to let formal examinations get in the way of good teaching.

Some of the main problems with language testing probably arise from the fact that many teachers dislike *testing* so much that they leave it in the hands of people who do not have much interest in *teaching*. If you work in a situation where you believe that change is needed in ELT and you want to work for that change, become involved in testing.

Change in an examination can have a bigger effect on teaching than any number of books about methods. However, a responsible attitude to change demands support for teachers who have been teaching to the old examinations. And that is another reason for not basing our teaching too solidly on examinations – they do change eventually.

Questions and activities

Think about your responses and then discuss them with a colleague if possible.

1 Look at some test items and ask yourself exactly what is being tested. To what extent does the test seem valid to you? What attempts have been made to standardize the marking?
2 Write some multiple-choice items of your own to test knowledge of vocabulary, grammar, and reading comprehension. Try out the items with colleagues or friends and find out if they agree or disagree with your correct choices and what they think of your distractors (wrong answers).
3 Construct a cloze test for a class you teach. Check the results against your intuitions regarding overall ability.
4 Have you ever failed an examination? What did you think about the teacher's role in your failure?

There is no key for this chapter because all the questions above are reflective or practical and depend either on experience or the materials found by each teacher.

11 PROFESSIONAL DEVELOPMENT

For some people, ELT is an occupation that may just last a few years. We hope that this book will be useful to them. But for a great many teachers, ELT is what they do throughout their working lives. We hope that, for them, this book has begun a process of reflection on experience that will afford them the satisfaction of knowing:

- why they do what they do
- how to express that knowledge to themselves and to others
- how to use their increasing awareness to take their careers forward.

Moreover, as in any job, years of routine and repetition can lead in time to feelings of boredom and demotivation – at its worst, a condition known as burnout. If this book succeeds in its aim of encouraging teachers to learn from their own experience, it might also provide a way of helping them to avoid the risk of burnout.

Whatever the stage of your career, the way forward, we suggest, is to become involved in a process of continuing personal and professional development.

Exactly what direction that development takes is not the point. You may wish to focus your development entirely on your work as a classroom teacher, or you may wish to get involved in materials preparation, course design, language testing, teacher training, or any other of the many different aspects of ELT at different times in your working life. The suggestion is, and research shows (Garton and Richards 2008), that being involved on a regular basis in some kind of small-scale developmental work is the one single factor most likely to help teachers go through their professional life with a sense of fulfilment and of a job worth doing.

In this section, we discuss some possible routes to such development: *reading, cooperation, exploration,* and *qualifications*. As you might expect, these are not entirely separate issues, but it is easier to talk about them under separate headings. Also, a different mix might appeal in different ways to different teachers.

Reading

A good way of supporting your development as a teacher is to read an ELT magazine or journal. Some well known ones from Britain are the *English Teaching Professional* and *Modern English Teacher*, both of which are mostly concerned with suggesting classroom procedures; the *ELT Journal* has longer articles with more space for discussion. From the USA, *TESOL Quarterly* presents much longer and usually more academic pieces.

All these journals offer subscribers access to an electronic archive of past issues, which can be searched for topics of interest. They also contain review sections that can help you decide which books you might want to buy. All of the above journals require a subscription, but there are also free Internet journals, of which probably the best known is *The Internet TESL Journal*.

Many more general ELT websites also offer short articles with practical tips. *Teaching English* has short introductory articles on a whole range of issues in ELT, as does *One Stop English*. There are thousands of websites for ELT; it is very difficult to select just a few. We would advise you to start with one and then follow the links!

At the same time, while you follow this global route, do not neglect your own local context. There may also be a local teachers' journal, or newsletters in your region, in which colleagues are trying to deal with exactly the same issues as you. This is something that is important for you to find out.

Cooperation

The most effective means of development for a teacher involve some kind of cooperation with other teachers. The most obvious form of cooperation involves attending each other's classes: an emotive issue which we raised in Chapter 1. If you have not tried the activity suggested there (Question 6, page 13), you might like to try it at some future stage.

The idea behind that style of observation is to distinguish it from assessment. By sharing your experience and giving you the chance to reflect on it, your observer has already helped enormously. If you want a more direct contribution, you could ask your colleague *Is there anything that you do with your students that you think would be relevant to what I am trying to do here?*

Notice that here the observer is still not being asked to evaluate what the teacher has done. That responsibility remains with the teacher him or herself. Of course, if you want criticism, praise, advice, or suggestions from your colleague, that is up to the two of you to negotiate.

A useful way to take observation forward is for the teacher to say in advance what the observer should look out for while watching the class. Some common examples of issues a teacher might want to raise are:

- Listen to how I give instructions and explanations and see if they seem clear to the students.
- Check if I involve all the students in the lesson, and how much.
- Listen for when I correct students and how I do it.

The observer is asked to concentrate on this issue in the lesson and to give feedback of the kind the teacher has asked for, whether that includes evaluation or not. The important point is to put an end to the isolation of teachers in their classrooms and to begin open cooperation in ways that teachers can feel comfortable with.

To take a broader view of cooperation, an important step towards continuing development is to join a teachers' association. The two main international ELT associations are the British-based International Association of Teachers of English as a Foreign Language (IATEFL), and the USA-based Teachers of English to Speakers of Other Languages (TESOL), whose addresses are given at the end of this book (page 201). There will almost certainly be a national association for you to join, and perhaps a more local teachers' group. The last of these is the most important for you to support, because this is where realistic responses to significant local issues can develop.

We made this point about supporting the local context when talking about reading. By the same token, just as the local newsletter might help support local collaboration and exchange of views, the international associations mentioned above also have their own house journals, *IATEFL Voices* and *Essential Teacher*, respectively, which aim to bring local concerns to a global audience.

It is also a good idea to join a virtual community of English teachers. Two useful sites are *Dave's ESL Café* and *TEFL.net*. The *English Teaching Professional* mentioned above also has an area for teachers to meet virtually and share ideas. Particularly for teachers involved in further study *Phil's EFL Support* is recommended. (See websites section at the back of this book.)

Exploration

You can extend your cooperation with a colleague into more serious exploration of your teaching. This would be a way to begin:

Keep notes on all the following stages:

1 Choose an area of your teaching that particularly interests you (for example, reading comprehension).

2 Focus on one small part of this area (for example, dealing with new vocabulary).

3 Explore what you do at the moment (for example, invite a colleague to watch you, make a recording, and explain to a colleague what was going on in the class, or ask your students what they most and least value about this part of your teaching).

4 Gather other ideas about this area of teaching (for example, talk to colleagues, read).

5 Plan something different from what you usually do and try it out, preferably with a colleague present, or with a recording.

6 Think about what happened and check your own impressions with those of a colleague and/or with your students. Try to express what you have learnt in writing if possible.

7 Decide whether to continue focusing on this area of your teaching or to move on to another.

8 Compare notes with other colleagues who are interested in classroom innovation and their own development.

9 Consider the possibility of running a workshop for teachers in your institution or locality.

Note the links between investigation, cooperation, and reading, as they all contribute to teacher development. Notice, too, the ways in which this procedure brings together knowledge from books, from experience, and from other people, while at the same time asking you to take responsibility for answering the question *What can I learn from all this?* and communicating your answer to your colleagues.

Exploration and cooperation are taken one step further when you share the results of your investigation of your own teaching with the wider community of ELT practitioners. There are many ELT conferences where you can present your work in the form of a talk or workshop. You could, for example, go to the annual international IATEFL or TESOL conferences. You can also check their websites for news of local conferences. Alternatively, or in addition to conference presentations, you can publish your work in one of the many teachers' journals, some of which we have already listed above.

You might think that your own exploration is only of interest to you, but you should not underestimate the communicative power of shared experience in professional development. It is also the case that editors are very keen to receive articles from teachers reporting on the above style of action research in context.

Qualifications

Qualifications are not necessary to development, of course. On the other hand, it could be advantageous to you to get a (further) qualification at various stages of your career. If this is the case, the most important thing to do first is to make sure that the qualification you are thinking of getting is recognized by the relevant authorities. Bear in mind that a degree from a foreign university, for example, may not be recognized in your national system.

ELT is offered in the state system of many countries as either the major or a subsidiary topic of a formal teaching qualification. People educated in this way have the advantage of knowing that they are gaining recognized certification, and of seeing their specialization in its broader educational context.

In addition to formal, full-time education, there are various short courses in the private sector that offer training of a variable standard. When it comes to choosing one, word of mouth may be the best recommendation. Any organization offering such a course should be able to put you in touch with someone who has recently completed it and can give you information and advice.

From a British perspective, there are two organizations whose qualifications are generally well thought of and recognized: Cambridge ESOL (a department of the University of Cambridge), and Trinity College, London, both of whose website addresses are given at the end of this book. The full range of their courses can be seen on those websites, but the core qualifications in each case are the Certificate and the Diploma.

The Certificate

This is usually an introductory qualification of at least 120 hours of tuition, often taken in an intensive four-week block. This certificate is generally for candidates with no teaching experience, and is seen as an initial qualification, after which graduates should be given on-the-job support. One might describe this as an 'apprenticeship' level. Some teachers of other subjects also use this qualification as a way of moving across to ELT; other, more experienced teachers use it as a way of updating their knowledge and awareness in a way that gives it official recognition. Certificates can also be obtained by distance learning, but you should look carefully at how the practical teaching component is organized. How will you be observed? What feedback will you get on your teaching?

The Diploma

These courses are usually of about the same length as the Certificate courses when taught in an intensive block, but they are often taught part-time over an academic year. They are aimed at experienced ELT teachers, usually graduates, who want to formalize and gain recognition of their expertise as independent professionals. They are also available as distance-learning courses.

Teacher Knowledge Test (TKT)

We stated in the Introduction that we kept the TKT in mind while writing this book. It is a relatively new qualification offered by Cambridge ESOL and it differs from the traditional Certificate and Diploma in some significant ways.

First, it is modular and any of the three modules can be taken in any order. Second, it is designed both for pre-service and experienced teachers. Third, it is tested only through examination – there is no formal teaching practice. If you are interested in this test, details can be found on the Cambridge ESOL website.

Going back to the state system, a large number of universities offer the following academic degrees in ELT.

Masters

Increasingly, getting a job in a prestigious institution, or getting a top job as a senior teacher or director of studies requires a higher-level qualification such as a Master's degree. In the British system, this usually means one year full-time, or two years' part-time study, although distance-learning options may allow you to extend the period. In the US American system, an MA can be obtained without prior experience. British universities are increasingly moving in this direction because of the greater number of full-fee paying students who can be recruited. The MA degrees in our field cover a huge range of possible content, and very different levels of ability might be regarded as satisfactory. Some MAs are little more than diploma courses, while others make demands that are equivalent to those of the early stages of doctoral study. Once again, you need to read the course prospectus very carefully and ask if you can be put in touch with graduates of the programme before you make a final decision.

The highest level of academic qualification is a doctorate. Some ELT professionals are taking this option, often because they find an area of particular interest during their Master's studies and decide to research it further. But it can also mean better job prospects, especially within a university system.

Whatever qualification you study for, make sure that you understand how you will be assessed, but do not allow that to dominate your thinking; give your tutors a chance to help you learn. Having said that, we conclude this section with some advice on the two probable forms your assessment will take.

Certificates and Diplomas should certainly have a *practical assessment,* where someone watches you teach; some MAs have this feature as well. These assessments sometimes take place outside your usual teaching context. If this happens to you, you should make every effort beforehand to get to know the students you will be teaching. It is also vital that you:

- know the assessment form your examiner is using
- talk to the examiner before the class about what you are trying to do, and after the class about how you think it went.

This last point is very important. Things can go wrong in anyone's class. An examiner will be impressed by a teacher who shows an awareness of what went well and what did not.

As far as the assessment form is concerned, discuss it with your colleagues and your tutors, and try it out on your colleagues' classes and on videoed classes if possible. The important part of this is the discussion afterwards, as you try to move towards an agreed idea of what constitutes good teaching.

Formal writing will also probably be a part of your assessment. In very general terms, examiners will want to see a response to two questions:

1 How do you act in a certain area of ELT?
2 Why do you think that is a good idea?

First, if you are writing to a given title, note that, in all probability, the title will suggest not only the required content of your answer, but also how you might organize it. Let us look at a possible example:

What are the advantages and drawbacks of groupwork?

Describe two techniques involving groups which you find useful with your students.

This suggests a section on 'advantages' which will explain the principles behind the desirability of groupwork. The section on 'drawbacks' will show an awareness of the difficulties involved in implementing these ideas. The 'two techniques' will involve different areas of language teaching and types of groupwork in order to show the breadth of your expertise. Your descriptions will show how you gain some of the benefits of groupwork while overcoming as best you can the difficulties of its implementation.

If you have time, you could add an introductory paragraph which tells the reader exactly how your response is organized and a final paragraph which summarizes the main points you have made.

Simply by following the wording of the question, you will be able to give a highly-organized response that will be very welcome to the (probably overworked) examiner. We recognize that this advice may sound somewhat simplistic, but writing under pressure can often be helped by simple, sound principles that are easy to remember.

Next, if you are free to choose your own topic for an assignment, choose a small one! Even if you are worried about how you can possibly produce as many words as the assignment demands, that is unlikely to be your problem once you start writing. We have never known anyone have a problem with a topic because it was too small. If you choose a topic such as 'Teaching writing', you will have no space in which to say anything specific to your teaching at all; you will find yourself simply repeating superficial generalizations.

If you choose a topic such as 'A peer-correction technique for an intermediate writing class', you should have the space to write about what you do
and discuss other possibilities you know about. This should help you keep a
focus on the principles and procedures of actual teaching, which is what your
examiner will want to see.

Organization is very important. Try thinking about what you want to say in
the following terms (adapted from Hoey 1983):

- *Situation*
  Setting – where you work, type and level of students, etc. and/or
  State of the art – what usually happens in a certain area of ELT.
- *Focus*
  Problem – something unsatisfactory about the situation, or some dif-
  ficulty that you face or have faced and/or *Purpose* – an aim or objective
  that arises or arose for you.
- *Response*
  Procedure – what you did, or what you intend to do about the problem
  or purpose and Principle – your reasons and arguments for the
  procedures.
- *Evaluation*
  Evidence – what data can you produce to show that your response was a
  good one? or Criteria – if you are writing about the future, how will you
  go about evaluating your response?

This is, of course, only one way of organizing a piece of writing. It is, however,
a very powerful one, and useful both for reader and writer. Just as we discussed in Chapter 9, (page 150) the use of an established pattern of textual
organization helps writers to present their ideas clearly and helps readers to
follow them.

Summary

This chapter has focused on your continuing development as a teacher. There
are strong links between what we are saying here about teachers and what
we said about learners and strategies in Chapters 1 and 2. What learners
and teachers have in common is the importance in their lives of *awareness*,
self-development, and *empowerment*. We have separated out certain potential
areas of development in this chapter. However these areas need to be worked
on together in order to be maximally effective. The overall argument suggests
that you cooperate with colleagues to explore your own teaching situation,
make your own discoveries, take responsibility for acting on them, and communicate the experience and its outcomes to others. You can support this

process by your reading and also by formal study. In this way, you may be able to walk your own unique path, engaged in a cyclical movement between experience and knowledge that will sustain you in your working life. It is a movement that we attempt to sustain in our own.

Questions and activities

This chapter is full of suggestions for teacher activity. The only real question is, 'What are *you* going to *do*?'

KEY TO QUESTIONS AND ACTIVITIES

Chapter 1

1 Learners' outside lives can be brought into class in many ways. Where course book activities use invented towns or places, the teacher can use the learners' own context. A classic example might be in a lesson on asking directions, to which learners can bring in maps of their own home town; or in an activity on comparatives comparing random countries, learners can be asked to compare their own countries.

2 Lightbown and Spada (2006: pp. 57–58) also discuss intelligence and aptitude (such as having a good memory), although the evidence from the research is inconclusive. Another characteristic of good language learners also seems to be not needing to understand everything and being able to tolerate uncertainty.

3 If you are interested in following up the opinions in the Lightbown and Spada questionnaire, there is a detailed account of the most recent research findings for each of the statements in Chapter 7 of their book *How Languages are Learned*.

4–5 These questions require your personal answers.

Chapter 2

1 Materials extract 2.4 relates to *strategies*. In this activity, students learn how predicting the content of a text can help with understanding it. (See Chapter 9.)

Materials extract 2.5 relates to *communication*. Students are asked to exchange personal experiences. There is also an outcome to be achieved, as they have to decide on the most interesting story.

Materials extract 2.6 relates to *practice*. In this case it is a controlled practice exercise on the use of definite and indefinite articles.

Materials extract 2.7 relates to *feelings*, as students are asked to describe situations that evoked particular feelings.

Materials extract 2.8 relates to *rules*, as students are asked to give the rules for the formation of the past simple tense.

2 Materials extract 2.6 also involves *communication*: understanding written texts is part of communication.

Materials extract 2.5 involves *practice* of the past progressive tense and of the contrast between the past simple and past progressive, as students are encouraged to use this form, as in *When did it happen? Where were you? What were you doing?*

Materials extract 2.6 could also involve inductive learning of *rules*, as students have the opportunity to see how articles are used in English.

3 In a *meaning to form* approach, students will start with communication activities such as the ones in Materials extracts 2.6 or 2.8, before moving on to rules and possibly practice.

In a *form to meaning* approach, students are likely to begin with rules, such as Materials extract 2.8, before moving on to practice and then communication.

Strategies could be found at any stage in either approach.

4 Good language learners are able to use and integrate all five strands described. For example, they:

- are prepared to risk making mistakes and they learn from the mistakes they make. This relates to communication.
- like to learn about the language. This relates to rules.
- They organize their own practice of the language. This relates to practice and strategies.

What other connections can you see?

Chapters 3, 4, and 5

There is no key for these chapters, as the answers to the questions are necessarily based on personal reflection and experience.

Chapter 6

5 Below is one suggestion for completing the lesson plan on pages 96–97 for the materials in Materials extract 6.2.

Teacher's activity	T↔S? S↔S?	Students' activity	Aim	Timing
5 Divide the class into two groups and assign roles. Ask students to say their part of the conversation along with the recording.	T→Ss	Repeat with the tape.	To practise stress, rhythm, and intonation.	11.32

Ask students to practise in pairs. Ask 1 pair to perform for the class.	T→Ss S↔S S↔Ss	Practise the dialogue. Repeat the dialogue.		11.47
6 Ask students to complete *Grammar Spot* individually. Explain any difficulties.	T→Ss S↔T	Complete the exercise.	To check understanding of key point and explain if necessary.	12.00
7 Ask students to ask and answer questions in pairs.	T→Ss S↔S	Respond.		
Ask one or two pairs to report back what they found out about their partner.	T→Ss S↔Ss		To practise the various uses of 'like'.	12.15
8 Play the recording and ask students to tick the correct answer.	T→Ss	Listen and answer.		
Ask students to compare answers in pairs. Play recording again if necessary.	T→Ss S↔S	Compare answers and listen.	To further practise the various uses of 'like'.	
Elicit answers from students. Ask students what key words helped them answer the questions.	T→Ss	Respond.		

Chapter 7

2 One of the best ways of making sure that a task is meaningful is to make sure that it has an outcome that the learners need to achieve. That way, the learners have a purpose for communicating which at least appears to go beyond learning the language. Consider the difference, for example, between saying to students on a Monday morning: *Get into pairs and talk about your weekend* and *Get into pairs and talk about your weekend. Find at least two things that you both did.* By adding a simple outcome, the communication has a purpose and is more personally meaningful.

Another way of making tasks more meaningful might be to base them on topics in which you know your students are interested. Or design the types of tasks that you know your learners might need to carry out outside the classroom. This is the case with business or workplace simulations for those studying English for their jobs.

3 A difficulty here is that one cannot be sure that the way competent users of a language go about carrying out a task will necessarily provide useful input for the students at their stage of learning. One certainly cannot take this for granted. The teacher needs to listen carefully to such recordings and make a judgement as to their usefulness. The basic questions to ask are:

    1 Will my students be able to follow easily what is said?
    2 Does the language represent the kind of speech that my students need to understand or to produce?
    3 Does the language include points of interest that my students need to be aware of?

Chapter 8

1 *Test your grammar* relates to communication, as students exchange personal information. It also relates to practice and rules, as students need to use particular verb patterns to complete the sentences.

Questions with 'like', exercise 1 relates to *communication*. It could also involve *feelings* if the teacher asks how the person found the experience or if the students themselves are studying in another country.

Questions with 'like', exercise 2 relates to *practice*, as the students have to put the correct sentences in the gaps and then repeat the conversation.

Grammar Spot implicitly relates to *rules*, as the students are asked to match the questions with their meaning and also to distinguish between prepositions and verbs.

Practice 1 relates to *practice* but also to *communication* as the students ask and answer questions about themselves.

Practice 2 relates to *practice*.

2 While teaching the materials the teacher will *provide security, encouragement,* and *guidance* to the students. In giving instructions and deciding on classroom management, he or she will be *organizing*. Before the students start an activity in pairs, the teacher might *model* an example with the students to be sure they know what to do. When students are working individually, or in pairs, the teacher will *monitor*. When students give the answers to controlled activities such as *Questions with 'like'* 2, *Grammar Spot*, or *Practice 2*, the teacher will give *feedback* on the students' language use, and possibly *inform*, if he or she feels the students need explanation of the language points being taught. The teacher will also be *motivating* students throughout; particularly in the personalized activities, the teacher can motivate them by showing an interest in the content of what the students say.

3 By doing the dialogue as a choral drill, students are more likely to keep the correct pace and rhythm, compared to practising it in pairs. It also takes some of the pressure off them to 'perform'. However, some students might struggle to keep up and give up all together. In the general chorus, the teacher might not notice difficulties that particular students are having.

By doing *Practice 1* as a group survey, the students will probably find the activity more interesting and motivating. In addition, the focus is then even more on *communication*. However, it will take longer than doing the activity in pairs, and the language use is less controlled.

Chapter 9

6 In both cases, we see a progression from more to less explicit teacher control of an activity. The learners move towards independent language use based on an internalization of what has been learned. Also in both cases the teacher attempts to guide and encourage learner initiative within the safe space that the teacher has structured.

Chapter 10 and 11

There is no key for these chapters, as the answers to the questions are necessarily based on personal reflection and experience.

GLOSSARY

accuracy: The production of spoken or written language which does not contain errors. If an activity is focused on accuracy, the learners pay attention to the correct form of the language.

acquire/acquisition: Internalizing of second language rules and vocabulary by using them, rather than studying them.

affix/affixation: Letter(s) added to beginnings or ends of words to change their meaning: e.g. *unhappy, movement*. See *prefix, suffix*.

aim: What the teacher and learners plan to achieve. This can be in a course or in a lesson.

appropriacy/appropriate/inappropriate: Language that is suitable/unsuitable for a particular situation.

assessment criteria: The standards against which learner performance in a test is judged.

blog: A personal record someone puts on their website, giving an account of their activities and their opinions.

circumlocution: Saying what you want to say in another way when you do not know the exact word or expression.

class profile: Information about learners in the class, including their age, nationality, previous learning experience, etc.

cognate: A word that has the same origin as another. For example, *house* in English/*Haus* in German.

cohesion: Ways in which sentences and phrases are linked to create connected text.

colloquial: Conversational, informal language.

concept checking: Ways of checking that learners have understood the meaning of new language.

connected speech: Spoken language in which individual words sometimes link up and change their pronunciation.

consonant: The English alphabet contains 26 letters. Apart from the five vowels *a, e, i, o, u*, all the other letters are consonants.

context: The background and situation in which we hear, read, or use language. Also, the words that come just before and after a word, phrase, or statement and help you to understand its meaning.

contextualize: Putting new language into a context so that the meaning is made clear.

continuous assessment: A system of giving a learner an overall mark/ grade based on work done during a course of study rather than on one or more final exams.

contraction: The short form of verbs as used in informal writing. An apostrophe is used to represent the missing letter(s), e.g. *Where's Harry? He's gone to London – he'll be back tomorrow.*

draft: A non-final version of a piece of writing which is later changed according to feedback given. When the learner makes the changes, he or she *re-drafts* the piece of writing.

elicit: Asking learners questions with the positive aim of discovering and demonstrating what they already know. For example, *Does anyone remember what we did last week?* Or *who can answer question 4?*

error: Inaccurate form or use of language.

exposure: When learners hear or read language for communicative purposes, without consciously studying it.

extension task: An activity that gives learners more practice in a particular aspect of the language under study.

extensive listening/reading: Reading a long text such as a short book or reader for pleasure, with attention to overall meaning. Compare *intensive reading.*

feedback: Response to what learners say and do, to give them an indication of how well they are doing.

flipchart: A piece of equipment that consists of a large block of paper fixed to a stand. The teacher can write on the paper and then tear off the top sheet.

fluency: The production of spoken language without unnecessary pauses, false starts, or repetition.

focus on form: When attention is paid to particular language forms, usually by identifying the form in context and then practising it.

functions: What we do with language, for example, apologize, explain, etc.

functional exponent: The way a function is expressed, e.g. *Would you like to …?* is an exponent for making an offer.

gap fill: An activity where students complete a text in which individual words are missing. This is often used to practise a specific language point.

goals: The overall aims that teachers and learners have.

graded readers: Books with a deliberately restricted level of language. These may have been written specifically for learners or be simplified versions of classic stories.

group dynamics: The behaviour of the learners in the class towards each other.

intensive listening/reading: Reading a short text with attention to detail. Compare *extensive reading*.

interlanguage: The rule-based language produced by a second language learner. It may have some features of the first language and some features of the second language. It continually changes as the learner revises his or her internalized rule system.

L1/L2: L1 is a learner's (dominant) first language, usually the one learnt as a child. This is sometimes also called the mother tongue. L2 is a learner's second language.

learner independence/autonomy: The ability of the learner to take responsibility for his or her own learning and to plan, organize, and monitor the learning process independently of the teacher.

learner profile: Information about individual learners such as age, L1, needs, preferred learning styles, etc.

learner training: Showing learners how they learn and teaching them learning strategies to increase their independence.

learning style: Each learner's preferred way of learning.

mingle (n and v): Activities where the whole class walks around and interacts.

model (n and v): An example of the language that the learners can copy. Teachers can also *model* language for learners.

monitor: To listen to the learners to see that they are on task, to check their use of the language, and to help them if necessary.

multiple-choice questions: Questions where the learners have to choose the correct answer from a number of possible answers.

needs: What the learner has to or wants to learn.

objective test: A test in which there are clear right/wrong answers.

open comprehension questions: Questions about a reading or listening text which students answer using their own words.

overhead projector (OHP): A piece of equipment that projects images onto a screen. The teacher writes on sheets of transparent plastic (overhead transparencies or OHTs) which are then used on the OHP.

peer assessment: When one learner or trainee evaluates another. Compare *self-assessment*.

peer feedback: When one learner or trainee gives feedback to another.

personalize/personalization: Making connections between the language being learnt and the learners' own lives.

phonemic chart: A table of the phonemic symbols used to represent meaningful individual sounds.

podcast: A digital recording made available on the internet and which can be downloaded to a personal computer or digital player.

prefix: Letter(s) added to beginnings of words to change their meaning, e.g. *unhappy*.

pre-teach: Teaching some aspect of a text, usually vocabulary, before the learners listen to or read it, in order to help them understand it.

process writing: An approach to teaching writing which focuses on the different phases involved, including planning, drafting, and re-drafting.

project work: An activity in which learners have to complete a large task, often consisting of a number of smaller tasks. Project-work usually involves creating a product, such as a poster, brochure, or radio broadcast, for example.

prompt: Helping learners to produce a word or sentence by asking them questions or suggesting words they could say.

rapport: The relationship between teacher and learners.

re-draft: See *draft*.

reformulation: A correction technique in which the teacher repeats the correct version of what a learner has said, but without pointing out the error explicitly.

register: Variation in style in which a person speaks or writes depending on the formality of the situation.

resources: All the materials that learners and teachers can use to obtain information about the language, for example, dictionaries, grammar books, websites, etc.

rhythm: The pattern of stress and syllables in spoken language.

scan: To read a text quickly to locate specific information.

self-assessment: When a learner evaluates him or herself. Compare *peer assessment*

self-correction: When a student corrects his or her own mistakes either spontaneously or with direction and support from the teacher.

skill: Each of the four major modes of communication – listening, reading, speaking, and writing. See *receptive skills* and *productive skills*.

skim: To read a text quickly to get the general idea or gist.

student-centred: When the focus of the activity is on the learners, who are given the opportunity to work together and express their own views.

subjective test: A test in which the opinion of the examiner plays a role in deciding the mark. This is the case with marking essays, for example. Compare *objective test*.

subskill: The four skills can be divided into subskills. For example, note-taking is a subskill of writing, and listening for gist is a subskill of listening.

suffix: Letter(s) added to ends of words to change their meaning, e.g. *movement*.

supplementary materials: Materials that the teacher can use alongside the main coursebook.

syllable: A unit of speech containing a vowel sound and usually one or more consonants, for example, *a*, or *cough*.

syllabus: A plan or programme for a course, specifying content, sequence, and sometimes methodology.

target language: The language that learners are aiming to learn, the L2. In a specific lesson plan, this may be a structure, a function, or lexis.

teacher talking time (TTT): Class time where the teacher is talking. At its best, this usually means giving instructions, giving feedback, etc. but at its worst it can mean the teacher taking up all the available time with his or her talk.

topic: The subject of a lesson, text, or activity.

topic sentence: This is the sentence, usually the first, that summarizes the main point of a paragraph.

transcript: A written copy of a spoken text (generally used after a listening task).

vowel: The English alphabet contains five vowels: *a, e, i, o, u.*

wiki: A type of website that allows a group of people to add, remove, or edit content.

word stress: This is where the emphasis is placed on one syllable in a word compared to the others, which are said to be unstressed, for example: *extremely*.

Acknowledgements

Some of these definitions are taken or adapted from *Teaching and Learning in the Language Classroom* by Tricia Hedge (Oxford Handbooks for Language Teachers), *Introduction to Teaching English* by Jill and Charles Hadfield (Oxford Basics), and *Oxford Advanced Learner's Dictionary*.

SOURCES AND FURTHER READING

Aston, G. (ed.) 2001. *Learning with Corpora*. Houston: Athelstan Publications.

Borg, S. 2008. *Teacher Cognition and Language Education: Research and Practice*. New York: Continuum.

Brown, H.D. 2007. *Principles of Language Learning and Teaching* (5th edn.). New York: Pearson Education.

Burns, A. 1999. *Collaborative Action Research for English Language Teachers*. Cambridge: Cambridge University Press.

Carter, R. and **D. Nunan.** (eds.) 2001. *The Cambridge Guide to Teaching English to Speakers of Other Languages*. Cambridge: Cambridge University Press.

Crystal, D. 2003. *English as a Global Language*. (2nd edn.). Cambridge: Cambridge University Press.

Cunningsworth, A. 1995. *Choosing your Coursebook*. Oxford: Heinemann Macmillan.

Davis, P., **B. Garside,** and **M. Rinvolucri.** 1999. *Ways of Doing: Students Explore Their Everyday and Classroom Processes*. Cambridge: Cambridge University Press.

Dörnyei, Z. 2001. *Motivational Strategies in the Language Classroom*. Cambridge: Cambridge University Press.

Dudeney, G. and **N. Hockley.** 2007. *How to Teach English with Technology*. Longman.

Eastment, D. 2007. 'Websites review: video.' *ELT Journal 61/1: 86–88*. Oxford: Oxford University Press

Edge, J. (ed.) 2001. 'Case Studies in TESOL: Action Research'. Alexandria, VA: TESOL Inc.

Edge, J. 2002. *Continuing Cooperative Development: A Discourse Framework for Individuals as Colleagues*. Ann Arbor, MI: University of Michigan Press.

Edge, J. (ed.) 2006. *ReLocating TESOL in an Age of Empire*. London: Palgrave.

Ellis, R. 2006. 'Current issues in the teaching of grammar: An SLA perspective' in *TESOL Quarterly 40/1: 83–107*.

Farrell, T. 2007. *Reflective Language Teaching: From Research to Practice.* London: Continuum.

Foster P. 1996. 'Doing the task better: how planning time influences students' performance.' In Willis J. and Willis D. (eds.) *Challenge and Change in Language Teaching.* London: Heinemann ELT.

Garton, S. and **K. Richards.** (eds.) 2008. *Professional Encounters in TESOL: Discourses of Teachers in Teaching.* Basingstoke: Palgrave Macmillan.

Graham, C. 2000. *Jazz Chants Old and New.* New York: Oxford University Press.

Harmer, J. 2007. *The Practice of English Language Teaching* (4th edn.). Harlow: Pearson Education.

Hedge, T. 2000. *Teaching and Learning in the Language Classroom.* Oxford: Oxford University Press.

Hoey, M. 1983. *On the Surface of Discourse.* London: Edward Arnold.

Hughes, A. 1989. *Testing for Language Teachers.* Cambridge: Cambridge University Press.

Johnson, K. 1996. *Understanding Communication in Second Language Classrooms.* Cambridge: Cambridge University Press.

Kachru, B.B. and **C.L. Nelson.** 1996. 'World Englishes' in S.L. McKay and N.H. Hornberger (eds.) *Sociolinguistics and Language Teaching.* Cambridge: Cambridge University Press.

O'Keeffe, A., **M. McCarthy**, and **R. Carter.** 2007. *From Corpus to Classroom.* Cambridge: Cambridge University Press.

Krashen, S. 1982. *Principles and Practice in Second Language Acquisition.* Oxford: Pergamon.

Kumaravadivelu, B. 2001. 'Toward a postmethod pedagogy' in *TESOL Quarterly* 35/4: 537–560.

Lightbown, P. and **N. Spada.** 2006. *How Languages are Learned. Oxford: Oxford University Press.*

Littlejohn, A. 1998. 'The analysis of language teaching materials: inside the Trojan horse'. In Tomlinson, B. (ed.) 1998. *Materials Development for Language Teachers.* Cambridge: Cambridge University Press.

McCarthy, M. 1991. *Discourse Analysis for Language Teachers.* Cambridge: Cambridge University Press.

McGrath, I. 2002. *Materials Evaluation and Design for Language Teaching.* Edinburgh: Edinburgh University Press.

McKay, S.L. and **N.H. Hornberger.** (eds.) 1996. *Sociolinguistics and Language Teaching.* Cambridge: Cambridge University Press.

McNamara, T. 2000. *Language Testing.* Oxford: Oxford University Press.

Morrow, K. (ed.) 2004. *Insights from the Common European Framework.* Oxford: Oxford University Press.

Nunan, D. 2004. *Task-based language teaching.* Cambridge: Cambridge University Press.

Phillipson, R. 1992. *Linguistic Imperialism.* Oxford: Oxford University Press.

Richards, J.C. and **W.A. Renandya.** (eds.). 2002. *Methodology in Language Teaching: An Anthology of Current Practice.* Cambridge: Cambridge University Press.
Richards, J.C. and **T.S. Rodgers.** 2001. *Approaches and Methods in Language Teaching.* (2nd edn.) Cambridge: Cambridge University Press.

Sinclair, J. and **M. Coulthard.** 1975. *Towards an Analysis of Discourse: The English Used by Teachers and Pupils.* Oxford: Oxford University Press.
Stevick, E.W. 1980. *Teaching Languages: A Way and Ways.* Rowley, MA: Newbury House.

Thornbury, S. 1997. *About Language.* Cambridge: Cambridge University Press.
Tomlinson, B. (ed.) 1998. *Materials Development for Language Teachers.* Cambridge: Cambridge University Press.
Tomlinson, B. (ed.) 2003. *Developing Materials for Language Teaching.* New York: Continuum.
Tsui, A. 2003. *Understanding Expertise in Language Teaching.* Cambridge: Cambridge University Press.

Ur, P. 1996. *A Course for Language Teaching.* Cambridge: Cambridge University Press.

Wenden, A. and **J. Rubin.** (eds.) 1987. *Learner Strategies in Language Learning.* Englewood Cliff, NJ: Prentice Hall International.
Willis, D. 2003. *Rules, Patterns, Words.* Cambridge: Cambridge University Press.
Willis, J. 1996. *A Framework for Task-based Learning.* Harlow: Longman.
Willis, D. and **J. Willis.** 2007. *Doing Task-based Teaching.* Oxford: Oxford University Press.
Windeatt, S., D. Hardisty, and **D. Eastment.** 2000. *The Internet.* Oxford: Oxford University Press.

USEFUL ADDRESSES AND WEBSITES

Teachers' Associations

IATEFL, Darwin College, University of Kent, Canterbury, Kent, CT2 7NY, UK
www.iatefl.org

TESOL, 700 South Washington Street, Suite 200, Alexandria, Virginia 22314 USA
www.tesol.org

For more information about teaching certificates and diplomas, contact:
ESOL Helpdesk, University of Cambridge ESOL Examinations, 1 Hills Road, Cambridge. CB1 2EU. UK. www.cambridgeesol.org
Trinity College London, 16 Park Crescent, London. W1N 4AH. UK.
www.trinitycollege.co.uk

Cambridge Teaching Knowledge Test Glossary

www.cambridgeesol.org/assets/pdf/tkt_glossary.pdf

TV and Newspapers

www.abc.net.au
www.bbc.co.uk
www.cnn.com
http://education.guardian.co.uk/tefl/
www.guardian.co.uk
www.mondotimes.com
www.gulfnews.com/home/

Publishers' Websites

Oxford University Press. www/oup.com/elt
MacMillan. www.macmillanenglish.com
Cambridge University Press. www.cambridge.org/elt
Pearson Longman www.pearsonlongman.com

ELT Websites

Dave's ESL Café. www.eslcafe.com
International House. www.ihes.com
One Stop English. www.onestopenglish.com
www.teachingenglish.org.uk
www.tefl.net
English Teaching Professional. www.myetp.com/
Phil's EFL Support. www.philseflsupport.com

Journals

ELT Journal. www.eltj.oxfordjournals.org
English Teaching Professional. www.etprofessional.com
Humanising Language Teaching. www.hltmag.co.uk
Modern English Teacher. www.onlinemet.com
TESOL Quarterly. www.tesol.org/tq
The Internet TESL Journal. http://iteslj.org/

Video Websites

TEFL.net. www.tefl.net
Video Jug. www.videojug.com

Testing

Council of Europe website with details of the European Language
Portfolio. www.coe.int/portfolio

Council of Europe website with details of Common European Framework
of Reference for Languages.
www.coe.int/T/DG4/Linguistic/CADRE_EN.asp

Cambridge website explaining how the Cambridge examinations are
mapped onto the Common European Framework. www.cambridgeesol.org

INDEX

Words in **bold** are included in the TKT Glossary